THE NAZIS

THE NAZIS

GEORGE BRUCE

CHANCELLOR PRESS

Published in 1974 by Hamlyn
© 1974 by Reed International Books Limited
This edition published in 1997 by Chancellor Press,
an imprint of Reed International Books Limited, Michelin
House, 81 Fulham Road, London SW3 6RB and
Auckland, Melbourne, Singapore and Toronto

ISBN 1 85152 698 6

Contents

Soldiers against Socialists

Kaiser Wilhelm II.

Germany embarked on the First World War with confidence and enthusiasm. War fever gripped the population. Crowds singing martial songs swarmed through the streets of Berlin. Catholic and Protestant priests invoked the aid of the Almighty in inspiring religious services. The avenues leading to Kaiser Wilhelm's palace were thronged with cheering mobs at all hours, and his briefest appearance brought outbursts of almost hysterical enthusiasm. War! It had come at last, and the Army, the Navy and the Kaiser were ready, anxious to show the world their strength and to win their laurels.

The reasons are easy to see. Germany possessed an arrogant monarch who saw himself as one of history's great military leaders, and the bulk of the nation agreed with this valuation. She also possessed a standing army of 870,000 men which was second to none in the world; a navy which was a challenge even to the sea-going might of Great Britain; a highly efficient industry; an overseas empire to which she was eager to add; and a middle class ideologically prepared for war by the Prussian military tradition and the writings of nationalist historians and philosophers.

Among these were notably the historian Heinrich von Treitschke and the philosopher Friedrich Nietzsche. Treitschke taught the theory of the all-powerful State and the grandeur of war. Through this alone, he argued, the individual could attain his highest fulfilment; for war was heroic and moral and the idea of perpetual peace was absurd. Nietzsche attacked Christian morality and values, called for the advent of the Superman, a creature beyond good and evil, and praised 'the will to war, to power, to conquest and revenge'.

The majority of Germans of the educated classes accepted these ideas, extreme as they are, because at that time they were the essence of Prussianism, and also because they believed war would be necessary for Germany to achieve her aim of dominating Europe and sharing with Britain in the colonial exploitation of the world's undeveloped territories. A philosophy of war and conquest freed them from moral scruples in the achievement of these aims.

Expansionism in Europe and overseas was the basis of German foreign policy in the years leading up to 1914. It was accepted without question by almost the whole population. When war came, fervent patriotism, a sense of Germany's special destiny among the nations and a belief in war as a heroic and moral way of achieving this destiny gave Germany her overbearing sense of power, her belief in ultimate victory and her cohesion during the four long years of war on two fronts.

Above: The 20-year-old Paul von Hindenburg (standing) poses in army cadet's uniform with his family, shortly before the outbreak of the Franco-Prussian war in 1870. Sixty years later he was to usher in the new Nazi Germany.

So the sudden announcement to the nation in October 1918 that Germany was trying to negotiate surrender terms, and that she had been defeated, dealt German pride a shattering blow. This was especially so because the first months of the fourth year of war had brought brilliant German successes: an advance to within 40 miles of Paris; the partial destruction of the British Fifth Army; the capture of 90,000 prisoners and 1,300 heavy guns; and the final defeat of both Russia and Rumania. Defeat seemed somehow inexplicable.

It had occurred in May 1918, after the failure of General Erich Ludendorff's second offensive in the battle of the Lys. When the German attack petered out through lack of reserves, and without having achieved its objectives, Marshal Foch struck back with powerful Allied armies reinforced by hundreds of thousands of fresh American troops, defeating the Germans at the second battle of the Marne, the third battle of Amiens, and the battles of St Mihiel, Meuse-Argonne Forest and Cambrai-St Quentin.

The first act of the drama that was to be so momentous

Right: Field-Marshal Paul von Hindenburg (left) and General Erich Ludendorff.

Overleaf: Some of the 33,000 German soldiers taken at Amiens in August 1918 enter captivity.

for the future of the German people now began to unfold. It was to provide the foundation upon which the Nazis would stage their own world-shaking tragedy.

Throughout the war years, Field-Marshal Hindenburg and his Chief of Staff, General Ludendorff, had dominated the civilian politicians through a War Cabinet of generals which had direct access to the Kaiser. By means of a quasi-military dictatorship the War Cabinet held the reins of

Friedrich Ebert (right), appointed provisional Chancellor after Kaiser Wilhelm II's abdication on 10 November 1918, was elected President of Germany's postwar Weimar Republic in February 1919.

power. In late September 1918, Hindenburg and Ludendorff gave the Kaiser the hideous and unexpected news of Germany's defeat and imminent military collapse, advising him to set in motion the formation of a ·representative civilian government to negotiate peace terms with the Allies. Ludendorff then resigned, having shouldered off on to the civilian politicians, whom he had denied any say in Germany's war policy, the appalling responsibility of dealing with its ruinous consequences. The Kaiser appointed Prince Maximilian of Baden to form a Cabinet and negotiate with the Allies.

German democracy, that fragile creature, was thus born again at the behest of the beaten generals and in the shadow of military defeat. Prince Max sought the cooperation of the Social Democratic Party to make his Cabinet representative and to satisfy Hindenburg and Ludendorff, for these fine old soldiers were anxiously looking round for a scapegoat to bear the blame for military defeat. The Social Democrats, their natural political enemies, exactly suited their purpose. For if they could be persuaded to enter the new coalition Government before peace terms were obtained from the Allies, it would be possible to shift the blame for the entire military surrender—what came to be called 'the stab in the back'—on to them.

Wise heads among the Party Executive warned against taking part in what could only be a government of grave-diggers. But they were ignored, and largely as an act of patriotism the Social Democrats decided to participate. With their cooperation Prince Max petitioned the Allies for an armistice on 3 October 1918. Meanwhile, in Germany, the shock of sudden defeat after four years of war

was making way for startling changes. First signs of unrest were a mutiny of sailors at Kiel in November, insurrection in industry, the formation of Workers' and Soldiers' Councils, the seizure of factories and a demand for the Kaiser's abdication to make way for the formation of a German Socialist Republic.

Prince Max and the Allies jointly announced the armistice terms during this revolutionary ferment. They included the evacuation by German armed forces of all occupied territory; withdrawal behind the Rhine; a neutral zone on the river's right bank; and the handing over of most of Germany's guns, aircraft and warships. An already threatening internal political situation was at once worsened by these terms. On 9 November the Berlin Workers' and Soldiers' Councils called a general strike in support of their demand for the Kaiser's abdication. Aware already that President Wilson of the United States had indicated that he would prefer to negotiate on behalf of the Allies with a democratic Germany, Prince Max advised the Kaiser to go. Wilhelm fled to the Netherlands on 10 November, where he was interned; Prince Max resigned in favour of the German Social Democratic leader Friedrich Ebert.

Thus ended the monarchy, against a background of revolutionary turmoil and anger, with industry at a standstill, the guns at last silent and the millions of dead rotting on the battlefields.

They were days of grief, bewilderment and collapse for proud, well-ordered Germany. Ebert gathered around him a provisional Social Democratic Government and accepted the armistice terms on 11 November 1918, a date still held sacred among the Allied nations as Armistice Day.

But two days earlier an event had occurred fraught with the gravest dangers for democratic government in Germany. Ebert had concluded a pact with General Wilhelm Gröner, Quatermaster-General of the Army, whereby Ebert ranged his Government behind the defeated generals against the Soldiers' and Workers' Councils, which were undermining their military authority. The effect of this was to legalize any action to suppress these Soviets in the armed forces.

For his part, Ebert received Gröner's assurance that he would safeguard the Government, by force if necessary, against Bolshevik revolution. Ebert, with Lenin's Soviet Russian triumphs fresh in his memory, had safeguarded the democratic Republic's life—but at the cost of eventual domination by armed forces controlled by the nation's most reactionary group. Gröner, only weeks after the virtual abdication of the German General Staff, had obtained for it the go-ahead for the reconstruction of the army, the new Reichswehr. It was an event which in time paved the way for the Nazi takeover.

Scarcely had Ebert taken power when he was faced by a revolt by the Communist Spartakist Union, backed by

Opposite, top: Revolutionaries of the Spartakist (Communist) Union in Berlin make preparations for their revolt against Friedrich Ebert's provisional Government in December 1918.

Opposite, bottom: Freikorps troops, aiding the Government during the 1918–19 Spartakist uprising, post a machine-gunner and riflemen in the shelter of rooftop statuary above Berlin's Brandenburg Gate.

Abtransport
gefallener Spartacisten.

Above: Rosa Luxemburg, the influential German Spartakist revolutionary, addresses a Socialist International meeting in Stuttgart before the war. In January 1919 she suffered the same fate as Karl Liebknecht.

Right: 'Peace! We attain it through Order!' This Government poster appeals for public order during the violent political upheavals of 1919.

Opposite, top: Medical orderlies, helped by a civilian, attend to the casualties of the bitter street fighting in Berlin between the Spartakists and the *Freikorps*.

Opposite, bottom: Karl Liebknecht, the German Spartakist revolutionary leader, harangues a huge Berlin crowd shortly before he was murdered by nationalists in January 1919.

the Workers' and Soldiers' Councils. In a desperate bid for power, they declared Ebert's Government deposed. Gustav Noske, Ebert's Defence Minister, appropriately a butcher by trade, faced with the probable total collapse of the regular armed forces, ordered the legalized volunteer military units, the *Freikorps*, led by unemployed ex-officers, against the Councils. Street fighting now followed. The Spartakist leaders, Rosa Luxemburg and Karl Liebknecht, were murdered, their shock troops defeated and the Communist bid for power narrowly averted.

Civil strife lessened temporarily, and in January 1919 elections for a new national assembly led to a coalition of the Social Democratic Party, the liberal Democratic Party and the Roman Catholic Centre Party. It took office away from revolutionary Berlin in the quiet little town of Weimar in February 1919, and set about the task of writing the new constitution for what became known as the Weimar Republic.

From now on, everything that occurred in Germany's political life seems, in retrospect, to have paved the way for the entry of the Nazis. First, the infant Republic, far from receiving deserved support, came under attack from both Left and Right in turn. In April 1919, the Communists and the Workers' and Soldiers' Councils seized Munich and established a Soviet. Gustav Noske's *Freikorps* crushed it after bitter street fighting which was repeated in several other towns throughout Germany.

Universal indignation was next directed at the blameless Government for signing, on 28 June 1919, the Treaty of Versailles, which, among other penalties, inflicted vast reparations of unlimited amounts upon Germany. It was,

as Alan Bullock remarks, 'looked upon as a fresh act of betrayal, and the Government was henceforward branded as an agent of the Allies in despoiling and humiliating Germany'.

In March 1920, the militarist extreme Right, led by the nationalist Dr Wolfgang Kapp and supported by Generals von Lüttwitz and Ludendorff, flung two *Freikorps* brigades into Berlin in a determined attempt to seize power. Ebert and his Government fled to Stuttgart, but not before giving the order for a general strike which stopped the city in its tracks. Faced with a city at a standstill, Kapp fled to Sweden. Counter-attack from the Left came once more in the Ruhr, Bavaria, Prussia and Würtemberg; only troops held in readiness saved the Government.

In the elections of June 1920, the very social classes who might have been expected to aid the Republic—the top ranks of the civil service, the professions and business—now withdrew their support for the Coalition's Democratic Party and gave it instead to the extreme right-wing German People's National Party. At the same time the Social Democrats lost votes to the extreme Left. Now that the administration was shorn of its power in the Reichstag, stable democratic government was impossible.

Extremism was now rampant throughout Germany, particularly in Bavaria and its capital Munich, which now became a haven for anti-Republican right-wing extremists, desperate ex-officers organized in so-called Patriot Leagues

General Franz Ritter von Epp, one of the founders of the
counter-revolutionary *Freikorps*, which crushed the
Berlin and Munich Soviets in 1919. He was to become
one of Hitler's secret supporters.

and Defence Leagues, with their secret arms caches and murder squads ready to gun down anyone who opposed them. An atmosphere of political terrorism flourished. It culminated in the murder on 25 June 1922 of Germany's outstanding Foreign Minister, Walter Rathenau, a Jew, by members of Captain Artur Ehrhardt's Consul action squad. Among these gunmen, characteristically, was a young naval officer, Erwin Kern, who was shot dead in a battle with the pursuing police. Like others of his generation he had be-

Above: Walter Rathenau, Jewish industrialist and German Foreign Minister, upheld the fulfilment of Germany's commitments under the Treaty of Versailles. He was assassinated in June 1922.

Left: General Walther von Lüttwitz, who commanded the rebel force which tried to overthrow the Weimar Republic in March 1920 and install a military dictatorship under Dr Wolfgang Kapp.

Below: Captain Arthur Ehrhardt (first left), a Marines officer and early supporter of Hitler, is escorted to his trial for implication in Rathenau's murder. He was acquitted of the charge.

come a victim of the defamatory propaganda which equated the Republic with the ruin of Germany and so-called Jewish domination.

Three days later the Government passed a Law for the Protection of the Republic, which made criminal offences of acts of violence or their condonement, as well as of anti-Republican conspiracy. But Bavaria's premier, Ritter von Kahr, now encouraged right-wing extremism by refusing to recognize the law.

At the same time, Major-General Ritter von Epp, Army Commandant in Munich, and his Chief of Staff, Captain Ernst Röhm, assured the ex-officers' organizations of continued aid and illegally supplied them with rifles, revolvers, hand grenades and ammunition, against the provisions of the Treaty of Versailles, which limited the German Army, the Reichswehr, to 100,000 men.

Of these days of menace, when Germany seemed to live on the brink of a volcano, John Buchan (later Lord Tweedsmuir) declared: 'The crust which we call civilization had worn thin and beneath could be heard the muttering of primordial fires.' This was particularly so in Munich.

To this city of despair over lost imperial power, of hopes for revenge and of ambitious military desperadoes, Adolf Hitler came early in 1919.

GESTAPO S.S. AND S.A
Nazi Instruments of Terror

Above: Hitler and Mussolini inspect an S.S. guard of honour in Berlin in 1937.

Right: S.A. trumpeters sound a call at the Nuremberg Rally of 1938.

The S.A. (*Sturm Abteilung*), or Stormtroopers, the S.S. (*Schutz Staffeln*), or Protection Squads, and the Gestapo (*Geheime Staatspolizei*), Secret State Police, were, with the concentration camps, the Nazi apparatus of terror and coercion for crushing all opposition – political, religious, social and military. The S.A., which was the first private army of the Nazis, was formed in 1921 by Captain Ernst Röhm, a war-scarred professional soldier to whom fighting was life. On Hitler's orders the Stormtroopers launched open terror by beating up audiences at rival political meetings so as to destroy opposition and create a wave of fear in Germany. By 1923 the S.A. was 15,000 strong, and ten years later it was 300,000 strong, with its own prisons and torture chambers, a threat to anyone merely overheard expressing doubts about Nazi policy as well as to 'Jews, Marxists and reactionaries'.

Hitler, never fully certain of the S.A.'s complete loyalty to him personally, formed in 1923 a Headquarters Guard (*Stabswache*), independent of the S.A., for his personal protection; and by 1925 from this and other most zealous and diligent Nazis the nucleus of the S.S. was formed. In black uniforms and caps, with death's head badges and black-bordered swastika armbands, they were organized in squads of ten as bodyguards and for security duties, including the suppression of Party revolts; they were also used for terrorism and for assassination. Later, the *Waffen-*

S.S. was formed and equipped with a full range of army weapons for similar military duties.

Under Himmler's leadership as *Reichsführer-S.S.*, the S.S. was expanded to a strength of 240,000 by 1939, later reaching more than a million, an élite of fanatical Nazis, trained to be merciless towards either subversive groups or so-called racial inferiors. Himmler saw these carefully chosen killers as the nucleus of a body of 'racially pure' supermen who would be the future rulers of Germany and Europe. Later, from 1937, they were merged with the police, selected members of which were admitted into the ranks of the S.S. The régime and discipline in the concentration camps was one of the duties of the S.S., who dealt with the prisoners there according to their own inhuman rules, without regard for legality. When Germany's Ministry of Justice objected to the many unexplained deaths in the camps, these objections were overruled.

In 1933 the Gestapo was formed specifically to handle political matters called 'anti-state tendencies', mainly opposition to or deviation from the Party line. At first under the control of the Ministry of the Interior, it was later made the entire responsibility of Himmler. It had the power to arrest and take into 'protective custody' anyone whom it pleased, and then send them without trial to a concentration camp for any period of time. Tyranny was thus total.

Top: S.A. 'old fighters' in their former uniforms at a rally in Berlin in 1934.

Above: An S.S. drummer whose kettle drums display the S.S. Death's Head emblem.

Left: The *Leibstandarte—Adolf Hitler* at a march-past. The prime characteristic of the S.S. was readiness to torture and kill in blind obedience to Hitler's orders.

Hitler's Beginnings

Left: Klara Hitler (née Pölzl), a woman of peasant descent. She died of cancer when Adolf was 19.

Right: Adolf's father, Alois Hitler, shows in this photograph something of the authoritarian personality which his son inherited.

The rise to power of the National Socialist German Workers' Party, or the Nazi Party, represented the triumph of Hitlerism. Nazism is thus inseparable from the ideas and personality of Adolf Hitler, although the beliefs of Nazism—anti-Semitism, anti-Marxism and extreme German nationalism—flourished before the advent of Hitler. Hitler gave these ideas their unique force and attraction, and wove them into a web that enslaved the entire German people and involved the world in war. Since it is impossible to separate Hitler and Nazism we should take a hard look at this extraordinary individual.

He was born on 20 April 1899 in Braunau-am-Inn, a border town in Upper Austria, where the Danube foams below the dark, forest-clad mountains and ruined castles gleam in the distance. Hitler was thus Austrian, not German. There were thorny patches in his parental background. His father, Alois, was a peasant, the illegitimate son of a peasant girl named Maria Schicklgruber who married a miller's hand named Georg Hiedler in 1842, when her son was five years old. Who Alois Schicklgruber's father was has never been established, but there is some evidence that he was Jewish. Maria Schicklgruber had worked in Graz for a family named Frankenberger, who are believed to have been Jewish, at the time she became pregnant. Hans Frank, Minister of Justice under Hitler, wrote in Nuremberg prison, after he had been sentenced to

death, that Hitler had instructed him to investigate in 1930 the question of his father's paternity, following allegations that he had been half-Jewish.

Frank confirmed the Frankenberger connection, adding that his inquiries showed that from the day of the birth of Maria's child Alois, Herr Frankenberger paid her maintenance on behalf of his own 19-year-old son for the next 14 years. A photograph of Alois, aged 40, with markedly Jewish features, lends weight to Frank's report. It possibly confirmed what Hitler already knew or suspected. The shame he would have felt over it suggests a reason for his virulent and murderous anti-Semitism.

Alois Schicklgruber, when he was aged 40 and an Austrian customs official, feared that the stigma of illegitimacy might hinder his advancement in the career that had taken him from the ranks of the peasantry to officialdom. In 1876, with the help of his late stepfather's brother Johann Hiedler, he persuaded the parish priest in the village of his birth that Georg Hiedler, whom he called Hitler, had accepted his paternity before his death some years earlier. The priest kindly amended the records so as apparently, but not legally, to legitimize Alois, in the name of Hitler.

The event, without legal basis, seems to be one of those strange turning points in history, as a result of which the apparently trivial is later seen to be momentous in its results. Did Alois Hitler clairvoyantly anticipate his future son Adolf's need for a surname with which more easily to spellbind the German people and the world? It is a strange possibility. For 'Schicklgruber'—especially 'Heil Schicklgruber'—would have been a grave obstacle to leadership of the Germans.

In 1885, when he was 48, Alois married Klara Pölzl, aged 25, granddaughter of Johann Hiedler, his stepuncle. Since Klara was now, apparently, his cousin—although no blood relationship actually existed—he nevertheless had to obtain a papal dispensation for the marriage. But Klara was pregnant, so the dispensation was helpfully expedited. Gustave, the first child, was born five months later and, like Ida and Otto who followed him, died in infancy. Adolf, the fourth child, was born in 1889; Edmund, who died when he was six, in 1894; and Paula in 1896.

The family was comfortably off on Alois' salary. After leaving primary school Adolf Hitler attended the Linz *Realschule* (more or less similar to a British secondary modern school). He wanted to be an artist, but his father urged him to try to become a civil servant. Conflict arose over the issue. 'My father forbade me to entertain any hopes of taking up the art of painting as a profession,' Hitler related in *Mein Kampf*. 'I went a step further and declared that I would not study anything else.'

This confession reveals at an early age Hitler's rigidity and lack of a spirit of compromise. As a schoolboy, he lacked, according to his teachers, any powers of self-discipline and concentration. He was talented in some ways, but lazy and hostile to either reproof or advice. Yet even then he wanted to dominate, and to be an outstanding leader.

Hitler's schooldays were to an extraordinary degree days of decision for him, Germany and the world. He would no doubt have become an architect had he done even the small amount of work needed to pass the certificate of education. But he failed to do even this, allegedly out of defiance of his father.

The more likely reason was that regular work of any kind repelled him. 'One thing was certain; my obvious lack of success at school,' he wrote later. 'What gave me pleasure I learned, especially everything which, in my opinion, I should later need as a painter. What seemed to me unimportant in this respect or was otherwise unattractive to me, I sabotaged completely.'

It was a narrow, egotistical attitude, but it became habitual to Adolf Hitler only to study or to inquire into things with which he was in agreement. Anything else he scorned, and either ignored, or later, when he had the power, suppressed. His history teacher, Dr Pötsch, awakened his interest in German nationalism and, by association, in history generally, yet even in this, his favourite academic subject, his record was mediocre because he failed to work systematically. There is no doubt that when his father Alois died of a stroke in 1903 he was gravely concerned about his son.

Klara, his widowed mother, left reasonably secure financially, now spoiled him by letting him leave school for a year on the flimsy grounds of an imagined chest ailment. Adolf hung around the house, spending his time sketching in an effort to persuade his mother to agree to his studying art. He showed extraordinary originality and boldness of outlook at this time by drawing, at the age of 14, ambitious plans for the entire rebuilding of Linz. Perhaps, if someone had then managed to convince him that academic study was worthwhile, architecture could still have become Adolf Hitler's profession.

But Klara Hitler exercised no control over her wayward and moody son. He returned to the *Realschule* for a year, and then left in 1905 without taking the certificate of education. His mother then agreed to his entering the Vienna Academy of Fine Arts, but in October 1907 Hitler failed the entrance examination and was advised by the director to try architecture instead.

Unwilling to acknowledge his failure, Hitler stayed on in Vienna, living the carefree life of an 'art student' with financial help from his mother, from whom he kept the truth of his failure. When she was gravely ill with cancer he still stayed on, with indifference to human suffering, even his mother's, returning home to Linz only for her funeral in December 1907, so that she never saw her son before her death.

He returned to Vienna in February 1908 with his share of his mother's small estate. This, and the orphan's allowance he received on the grounds that he was a student at the Academy, amounted to 83 Kronen a month. It was more than a junior teacher's salary and enabled him to live on in Vienna, sharing a room for the next four months with his friend from Linz, August Kubizek, who had begun studying seriously at the Vienna Conservatoire of Music. Hitler's overwhelming passion for the romantic and heroic themes and music of Wagner's operas had already developed, and the two spent many of their evenings together at the Vienna Opera House; but he had no other friends, and though he was apparently attractive to girls he showed no interest in them. Love left him cold, and sex at this time seemingly repelled him.

He once more sought a place in the Academy in September 1908, but was again rejected. Admittance at the School of Architecture was impossible without first having studied at the Technical College's building school; and this required the certificate of education, which he had not studied enough to take.

The event became a turning point in his life. He gave up his art student role, went to live in a dingy hostel, disappeared in Vienna's teeming social underground, and began painting copies of picture postcards for a living. A down-and-out named Reinhold Hanisch whom he met there peddled them for him, to make a little money for them both. 'There were days when he simply refused to work,' Hanisch said later. 'Then he would hang around night shelters, living on the bread and soup that he got there, and discussing politics, often getting involved in heated controversies ... Whenever we had a particularly good day, on which we earned a lot, he would disappear for a whole week.'

At first Hitler hardly knew what the political arguments were about. 'The word Marxism was as yet little known to me, while "Social Democracy" and Socialism seemed to me identical concepts,' he wrote in *Mein Kampf*. '... But now, at one stroke, I came into contact with the products of its education and "philosophy". And in a few months I obtained what might otherwise have required decades! An understanding of a pestilential whore, cloaking herself as social virtue and brotherly love ...'

This hatred of Social Democracy was one of the main foundations of the political philosophy Hitler unconsciously had started to develop. He hated Social Democrats, Marxists, trade unionists, parliamentary democracy and, above all, Jews.

The great discovery of his life, to which he clung with all his demonic power, was that the Jews had formed a

Adolf Hitler, aged 12 months, takes a thoughtful look at the future.

conspiracy to destroy the 'Aryan' race—of whom the Germans were the essence—by means of 'race defilement', Bolshevism and Social Democracy. 'When I recognized the Jew as the leader of Social Democracy the scales dropped from my eyes. A long struggle had reached its conclusion.' From then on his hatred of Jews increased daily until it became an insane fury which distorted his character. Soon not merely Jews but 'world Jewry' became the target for this hatred, coupled dangerously with the growth of a fanatical German nationalism which later grew into a powerful ingredient of Nazi expansionism.

To these irrational hatreds, the youthful Adolf Hitler was adding a sketchy political education obtained from newspapers, from the debating sessions of the Austrian parliament, from voracious reading of library books and from the political pamphlets he bought on the Viennese bookstalls. These were published mainly by Georg von Schoenerer's anti-Semitic German National Party, and Dr Karl Lueger's lower-middle-class Christian Social Party, in whose title 'Christian' had sunk to the level of a euphemism for anti-Semitic. Hitler admired the propaganda of both these parties, but it was the Social Democrats who opened his eyes to the power of violence and physical terror as a political dynamic. The mass organization of the Social Democrats astonished him: 'For nearly two hours I stood with bated breath watching

the gigantic human serpent slowly winding by,' he said of one of their workers' rallies.

Hitler seems to have been influenced greatly by the popular pseudo-scientific theories of Aryan and Teutonic racial supremacy, notably those of the Frenchman Count Joseph de Gobineau (1816–1882), the naturalized Englishman Houston Stewart Chamberlain (1855–1927), and the German composer Richard Wagner (1813–1873).

De Gobineau contended that while the white races created civilization, it could not exist without the genius of the Aryan and, in particular, the German race. Houston Stewart Chamberlain argued in *Foundations of the Nineteenth Century*, a book which ran to eight editions in Germany, that race is the vital factor in history, that the Jews are a danger to the Teutonic race and that the Teuton is the soul of European culture. In 1923 this popular figure in Germany was to write to Hitler: 'With one stroke you have transformed the state of my soul. That in the hour of her deepest need Germany gives birth to a Hitler proves her vitality ...'

Hitler was also fascinated by Wagner's musical world of gods and heroes. Wagner attacked the Press, democracy and Jews as a danger to the spirit of the German race, which he idealized as the saviour of civilization.

These Viennese days also gave Hitler his own sinister assessment of human psychology. He learned to put the lowest value on human motivation and never to forget the power over it of fear. In the lodging houses and the soup kitchens of that carefree, cosmopolitan city he also learned never to trust or commit himself to anyone, to be amoral in his readiness to cheat and lie, and to be unscrupulous and, if necessary, ruthless in realizing his aims. He won himself a distorted view of human nature, social life, history and politics with this misdirected, unbalanced self-instruction. But he had learned thoroughly what he had needed to reinforce his hatreds and his primitive lust for power.

'In a few years,' he related in *Mein Kampf*, 'I thus fashioned for myself the essence of the knowledge upon which I still rely. In that period I created a world outlook and a philosophy which has become the granite foundation of my deeds. I had only to add a little more to the knowledge which I had gained then. I did not have to change anything.'

A stupendous claim, it illustrates the kind of man Hitler was becoming—one of recondite knowledge, and of a demonic power that would grow until it would possess him utterly and enable him to dominate Germany.

But destiny of a different kind caught up with him in 1913. For three years he had evaded his obligation to register for Austrian military service at the age of 21; and in May 1913, possibly to avoid arrest, he uprooted himself from the Vienna hostel, quit Austria altogether and went to live in the German city of Munich. There he improperly registered himself as a stateless person, most likely so as further to evade the Austrian draft; and also, in the event of war, to serve with the German Army rather than under the Habsburg Empire which he so much hated.

But the Austro–Hungarian authorities moved swiftly and traced him to Munich. Visited by the police, he was

Above: Adolf Hitler, aged ten (centre, top row), poses in 1899 with his teacher and class mates of the primary school at Leonding, near Linz, Austria.

Right: George von Schönerer, seen here during a brief stay in prison, greatly influenced the development of Hitler's Nazi philosophy.

in danger of arrest, extradition and imprisonment. He wrote to them denying that he had tried to escape the call-up, pleaded sickness and was permitted to register in nearby Salzburg. There he was ruled physically unfit to bear arms. For the next 14 months he lived partially by peddling his drawings and paintings but mostly on money he had obtained from his aunt, Johanna Pölzl, a hunchback employed as a domestic servant in Austria.

It was a miserable life, without hope or promise, for despite Hitler's argument in *Mein Kampf* that he spent his days as a builder's labourer and studied industriously in his spare time, there is no evidence to support it.

The outbreak of the First World War in August 1914 was a godsend for him. Like many other rootless young men of his kind, he greeted it with emotions of self-interest as well as of patriotism. 'I am not ashamed to say,' he wrote later, 'that, overcome by stormy emotions, I fell down on my knees and thanked heaven out of an overflowing heart for granting me the good fortune of living at this time.'

Not wishing to fight for Austro–Hungary, he petitioned King Ludwig III of Bavaria to allow him, an Austrian, to fight in a Bavarian regiment in the German Army. Permission was quickly granted and he enrolled in the

16th Bavarian Reserve Infantry Regiment, which Rudolf Hess, and then Max Amman, who became the Nazi Party business manager, had also joined. In October 1914 it fought in Crown Prince Rupprecht's Sixth Army as part of the Sixth Bavarian Division in the first battle of Ypres. Then and later, Hitler was a despatch runner attached to regimental headquarters, a dangerous and solitary task which suited his temperament and which he was reported to have carried out 'with distinction'.

He was promoted to corporal – 'that hysterical fellow will never make an officer,' said his captain – and awarded the Iron Cross (Second Class), the Distinguished Services Military Cross (Third Class) and finally, a rare distinction for a corporal, the Iron Cross (First Class) in August 1918. Wounded at the battle of the Somme in 1916, he was also

gassed during a British attack in October 1918 and trans-ferred to military hospital in Stettin.

There, in November, he heard the news of the Kaiser's abdication and of what was, to him, Germany's incredible surrender. This he immediately attributed to the machina-tions of Jews and the so-called 'November criminals' among the politicians – never to the army's high command, Field-Marshal Paul von Hindenburg and General Erich Luden-dorff. In view of all that the army had come to mean for him, one can well believe his account of his emotional reaction at the news. 'Everything went black before my eyes; I tottered and groped my way back to the dormitory, threw myself on my bunk, and dug my burning head into my blanket and pillow.'

He was moved principally by the feeling that the

sketchy political ideas he had acquired in Vienna, this military emphasis formed the psychological basis of the Hitler who would create the Nazi Party.

He was struck now by the social and revolutionary turmoil sweeping through Germany, failing to see it at best as a welcome democratic upsurge against the military autocracy which had brought the nation to ruin. More than ever he was dominated by the 'Jewish–Marxist stab in the back' hatreds. But he saw that Germany was nearing the political crossroads at which her future would be decided.

He made the great, irrevocable decision of his life, that he would 'go into politics'.

It was a mere statement, because he had not the remotest idea of how to go about it. He was a corporal in 1918, doing occasional guard duties in Munich. 'At this time,' he related, 'plan after plan went through my mind. For days I wondered what could be done, but the end of every meditation was the sober realization that I, nameless as I was, did not posses the least basis for any effective action.'

Now, unexpectedly, the door into the world of politics opened for Hitler of its own accord.

Communist revolutionaries in this chaotic postwar period were trying desperately to subvert the troops, whom they saw as the sole obstacle to a seizure of power in Germany. Captain Karl Mayr, head of Press and Propaganda in the Reichswehr Group H.Q. No. 4 (Bavaria), decided to oppose the Communists by placing trained nationalist agents in the Army to spread patriotic and conservative sentiments. Hitler, who had already given useful evidence to a military inquiry about subversion in the ranks, was sent in June 1919 on a course for training in this work.

He felt he was walking on air when he received the assignment. Awkward and gauche though he was, he soon won marks as an orator, startling to all who saw him, his gaunt features and hypnotic blue eyes staring below the lank lock of black hair dangling over his receding forehead. A confidential report called him 'a born demagogue; at a mass meeting his fanaticism and popular appeal compel the attention of his audience'.

So impressed was Mayr that he began to seek Hitler's advice on propaganda matters, making him an unofficial member of his staff and an informer on the policies and ideologies of the political groups and parties which then teemed in Munich.

The turning point in Hitler's life came one day in September 1919. He went to report on one of the smallest parties, the German Workers' Party, which met in a room in the Sterneckerbräu, a cheap, smoky tavern in old Munich. It was an assortment of middle-class nationalists and anti-Semitic malcontents, more like a discussion group than a political party, and had been founded by a railway

tremendous sacrifices had all been in vain, but he was no less overcome by the thought of saying goodbye to the German Army, which had become his home and his way of life, giving it meaning for the first time. He had no other home, no wife, no family, no job to go back to.

Hitler had now become in spirit a regular soldier to whom the military life was all. If he disliked the army's boisterous camaraderie, he appreciated its comradeship, its system of military discipline, and good order, rewards and punishments, rank and values. He felt he belonged instead of being the rejected outsider he was in civilian life.

In addition, military organization, with its emphasis on leadership and its delegation of authority from commanding general all the way down to the most humble N.C.O., had moulded his thinking permanently. Together with the

mechanic, Anton Drexler, aided by Karl Harrer, a journalist. Dietrich Eckart, a writer with a little money of his own, was associated with them.

Konrad Heiden, who witnessed the birth of Nazism, tells in his biography of Hitler how Eckart expounded ideas on the kind of man the new party needed for a leader. 'He won't wince at the rattle of a machine-gun,' he declared. 'The rabble must be given a damned good fright. An officer wouldn't do; the people don't respect them any more. Best of all would be a workman in a soldier's coat with his tongue in the right place.

'He needn't be very brainy; politics is the most imbecile business in the world and every market woman in Munich knows as much as those fellows in Weimar. I'd rather have a stupid, vain jackanapes, who can give the Reds a juicy answer and not run away whenever a chair-leg is aimed at him, than a dozen learned professors who sit trembling on the wet trousers-seat of facts. He must be a bachelor! Then we shall get the women.'

The pattern might have been almost tailor-made for Hitler at that time.

He spoke at the meeting, galvanized the little group, and was invited to join it and have a place on its committee. With Mayr's agreement he did so, becoming Party Comrade No. 55 and the seventh member of the executive committee. From the start, at meetings in Munich's cheapest beer cellars, Hitler became its main speaker and attraction, with his raucous and frenzied denunciations of 'the Berlin Jewish Republic', 'the November criminals' and 'the Weimar traitors'.

The lie that Ludendorff had so carefully fostered, that the democratic politicians were guilty of Germany's defeat, had already become a legend.

The Nazi Party was about to be born. In January 1920 Hitler, already the dominant member of the infant group, was elected head of propaganda.

Below: Dietrich Eckhart, a writer of anti-Semitic views, was one of the Party's earliest members. He became Hitler's guide, philosopher and friend, exercising a considerable influence upon his intellectual development.

Opposite, top: Anton Drexler, a tool-maker who founded a patriotic workers' party to combat the Moscow-dominated Left. Launched in March 1918 as the German Workers' Party, it became, after Hitler seized control, the National Socialist German Workers' Party, or Nazi Party.

Opposite, bottom: Lieutenant Hermann Goering, photographed in France in 1916. He had a distinguished record as a fighter pilot, commanding the famous Richtofen squadron in 1918. Like many ex-officers in postwar Germany, he was strongly attracted to the infant Nazi Party.

Below: Corporal Hitler poses with wounded comrades in military hospital in October 1916. He served in the front line for four years, was wounded on the left thigh in 1916 and gassed in 1918.

THE LEADERS
Paladins of the Third Reich

SPEER

The story of Albert Speer is the tragedy of a brilliant man who could have become a world figure in his profession outside Nazi Germany. Instead, as Reich Minister for Armaments and War Production, he grew to be second only to Hitler, and then served 20 years in Spandau gaol.

Nonconformist to the end, Speer displayed open contempt for the social misfits of the Nazi hierarchy, personally blocked Hitler's orders in 1945 to destroy Germany's industrial fabric in a scorched-earth policy, and at Nuremberg was the only top Nazi to admit his guilt.

The son of a successful architect in the industrial town of Mannheim, Speer was born in 1905 into a cultured upper-middle-class German family. He qualified as an architect in 1927 and joined the Party in 1931 after attending one of Hitler's meetings. 'I was not choosing the Nazi Party,' he said later, 'but becoming a follower of Hitler, whose magnetic force reached out to me the first time I saw him.'

For this intensely ambitious young technocrat it was the only alternative to emigration, for there would have been little work for him outside the Party ranks, and he made his choice thinking he could play a non-political role. It was a pathway to power and wealth, but the most fateful move of his life.

Taken up by Hitler in 1933 after he had redesigned the decaying old Reich Chancellery, he became before he was thirty the Führer's undisguised favourite, and began to carry out his grandiose building schemes in Berlin, Munich and Nuremberg. Speer sold his soul completely, made his great talents the vehicle for Hitler's ponderous neo-classical architecture and gave Hitler an outlet for his longings in this field.

In return the Führer opened the Party's innermost circle to him, awarded him the coveted Golden Party Badge, all the material rewards the Reich could offer – and a much cherished watercolour painted in his Vienna days. Speer, obsessed by his own spectacular triumph, repressed his misgivings about anti-Semitism, concentration camps and the blood the Nazis were spilling across Europe.

Appointed Armaments and War Production Minister in 1942, he achieved a fabulous rise in output in 1943 and though largely the result of slave labour it enabled Germany to stay in the war. In 1944 he committed himself to an opposition group and personally planned an attempt on Hitler's life. For technical reasons it was abandoned. Speer was released from Spandau in October 1966.

BORMANN

Martin Bormann was the only top Nazi to escape. After Hitler's death on 30 April 1945, he vanished into Berlin's shell-torn streets and is still being hunted today. This mysterious end is entirely in keeping with Bormann's manner of life, which was dedicated to achieving power without glory.

Bormann rose from obscurity to a place in the hierarchy second only to Hitler himself, who defended him against the attacks of other Nazi barons. 'There is sense in everything he does and I can absolutely rely on my orders being carried out by Bormann immediately and in spite of all obstacles,' he declared. 'With him I deal in ten minutes with a file of documents for which with another man I would need hours.'

Bormann first appeared in the Hitler circle as personal secretary to Rudolf Hess, who was then head of the Party Chancery. After Hess's flight to Britain in 1941, Hitler appointed Bormann in his place. Bormann made himself a man the Führer could not do without. He began to make the decisions as to who could – and who could not – see the Führer, and who should be present at important meetings, thus making more enemies than friends. Soon he administered Hitler's own financial affairs, keeping a tight rein on expenditure, even doling out Eva Braun's modest allowance. Speer, who like most of the other top Nazis hated him, tells how Bormann solved Hitler's financial problems permanently in 1933 by arranging with the Minister for Posts for a copyright

fee to be paid to Hitler for the right to reproduce his picture on all German postage stamps. The money cascaded into the Führer's treasury.

When Bormann became Hitler's personal secretary in 1941 his power increased tenfold and he dominated the Party's administrative machinery. He also dominated the perpetual power struggles that raged in the top Nazi echelon, defeating in turn Goering, Goebbels and Himmler. This short, squat man, with a bundle of files invariably tucked under the arm of his ill-fitting civil servant's uniform, was a tough and relentless Nazi through and through. 'Even among so many ruthless men, he stood out by his brutality and coarseness,' Speer noted. 'A subordinate by nature, he treated his own subordinates as if he were dealing with cows and oxen. He was a peasant.'

Jealous of the enormous power he had won and frightened of losing it, he never left the Führer's side for more than a decade. And when at last he vanished, the Nazi drama had ended and the Führer's corpse was in flames outside the Bunker.

GOERING

Goering's tragedy was Britain's good fortune. For had the corpulent Field-Marshal striven with the same outstanding ability as C-in-C of the Luftwaffe and Minister For Air as he had done six years before as Reich Prime Minister, the course of the war would have been very different. But Goering was past his best even before the first shots of the Second World War were fired in Poland. Drugs, gluttony and slothfulness – the moral and physical corruption of Nazism – had done for him.

Born in 1893, in his twenties Goering was one of Germany's outstanding First World War fighter pilots, with 22 kills to his credit and the top decoration, *Pour Le Mérite*, when he succeeded Baron von Richthofen as commander of the Richthofen 'Flying Circus' of fighter aces. He was attracted to the Nazis by their violence and dynamism, was enrolled joyously by Hitler and soon given command of the Stormtroopers. Goering quickly displayed a crude talent for civil warfare, then rife in Germany. 'Shoot anyone who makes difficulties!' he ordered during the Munich beer-hall putsch. But, with a bullet in the groin, Goering himself was shot, and he went into exile in Sweden until 1926, returning when Hitler was again on the road to power.

By 1933 he had become the second man in Germany. As Prussian Minister of the Interior, he filled key posts in the police with S.S. and S.A. men, advising them to 'make use of firearms . . . without regard to the consequences . . .' He established the first concentration camps, for Jews and political opponents, and made Himmler head of the Gestapo.

In the war, fury at his pilots' failure in the Battle of Britain led him to launch terror bombing on London and Coventry, instead of concentrating solely on industrial targets, which if effectively done could have floored Britain. By mid-1942, according to Albert Speer, he had lapsed into a kind of bemused lethargy, hunting at his estate Karinhall, toying with his collection of looted art, designing grandiose new uniforms.

His supreme—and last—act of folly was his promise to Hitler that the *Luftwaffe* would supply the Army at Stalingrad, although his Staff had already established that this was impossible. But Hitler relied on it, failed to retreat when his forces were still intact and suffered a disastrous defeat. Even the Führer's confidence in him evaporated after this debacle.

In 1943 Speer observed his 'lacquered fingernails and obviously rouged face. The oversized brooch on his green velvet dressing gown was a familiar sight.' Soon Goering's irrational behaviour had lost him all respect in Germany.

He was sentenced to death at Nuremberg, but poisoned himself with cyanide in his cell. His looted art collection was afterwards valued at £20 million.

GOEBBELS

To Dr Joseph Goebbels, Minister of Propaganda and Public Enlightenment in Nazi Germany, belonged the distinction of fabricating the semi-religious cult of Führer-worship that lay at the heart of Party doctrine. To the clumsy, hesitant, maladroit and uncertain Hitler of the early days Goebbels gave the public image of a heaven-sent man of destiny who had come to save the nation in its darkest hour. 'Like a servant of God he fulfills the task which was given to him and he does justice in its brightest

and best sense to his historical mission,' he wrote in his diary. And in *Der Angriff*, his newspaper: 'What diligence and knowledge and school learning cannot solve, God announces through the mouths of those whom he has chosen. Genius in all fields of human endeavour means—to have been called. When Hitler speaks all resistance breaks down before the magical effect of his words.'

Such was the trend of Goebbels' public speeches and articles in the 1920s and 30s—apparent awe in contemplating the redeemer who had come to save his people. With all the media—press, radio, films, publishing and theatre—forced to be vehicles for Nazi doctrines, he created around Hitler a messianic aura which disarmed all opposition and led Germany and Europe to disaster.

Joseph Goebbels, who was born in the Rhineland in a humble family, had worked hard at grammar school and studied literature and philosophy at Bonn, Freiburg and Heidelberg universities, taking his Ph.D., in 1920, joining the Nazis in 1922 after failing as a writer and journalist. The very antithesis of the Nazi ideal of the robust, blue-eyed German, he was small and dark, with a deformed foot, upon which he hobbled lamely. He compensated for these shortcomings with a feverish drive for power and prestige. He gained it partly in 1931 when he married the wealthy Magda Quant, and made their Berlin home an unofficial headquarters for the venerated Leader; and partly in 1933, when he became Reich Minister of Propaganda. He allowed no moral scruples to hinder his brilliant creativity in this field, and he dominated the propaganda content of Germany's entire communication media. However, his power rested principally on his ability to project the image of the omnipotent whether in victory or in defeat.

HIMMLER

He prided himself on his love for small furry animals and birds. He was a very ordinary looking man with a pince-nez, small blue eyes, soft white hands threaded with fine blue veins, and sloping shoulders. As a young man he took an agricultural diploma, then, because he was not strong enough for the rigours of small farming, became a chicken farmer. His family background was that of the respectable German middle class; his

father was a schoolmaster and his grandfather was a police president, both of them rigid authoritarians who brought up their respective sons to be devout Roman Catholics. An unlikely beginning for the man whose name became almost a synonym for terror in Europe.

But if this is not strange enough, Heinrich Himmler's own character as a young man showed not a hint of the sadism and brutality—the lust to destroy which distinguished him as Minister of the Interior and *Reichsführer-S.S.* Indeed, it was unremarkable to the point of the commonplace. How then did he become the monster that he did? What changed him, so that he quite cheerfully and with a fine sense of moral rectitude launched the concentration camps, with their régime of flogging, hanging and the tanning of human skin for lampshades; the S.S. torture cells, with their terrifying apparatus for extorting confessions: the pseudo-scientific experiments on men and women prisoners; the Gestapo, and the shadow of terror it cast across all occupied Europe; the campaign for the murder of the entire Polish intelligentsia and the extermination in the gas chambers of every Jew his agents could lay hands on?

The first reason is that probably as a result of his defective relations with his father Heinrich Himmler lacked that vital sense of being human which normally unites men and women of all degrees, cements civilized society and enables it to function. Secondly, from his earliest years Himmler had learned a respect for authority so unquestioning and complete that it had forged in him a fanatical will in this regard which dominated him entirely, so that even marriage, for example, had no meaning for him, and he deserted his wife.

The third reason is that he met and was more or less hypnotized by Hitler, who saw in him a perfect tool for attaining power through terrorism. Winning the Führer's trust, he was given the task of creating the S.S., that inhuman embodiment of Hitler's will and the Nazi pseudo-mysticism which Himmler worshipped. Soon Himmler controlled the entire complex of police power in the new German empire. It gave him the power of life and death over some three hundred million people.

Before he killed himself by swallowing cyanide after his capture by the British in May 1945, this misguided Nazi romantic had taken the lives of several million people in the determined belief that the dead were part of the foundations of the Nazi New Order.

The Birth of Nazism

A demolized German army officer, shorn of his left leg,
accepts a few coins from a passer-by in an effort to
survive by begging in Germany's postwar economic crash.

Opposite page: Some of Germany's six million
unemployed loiter destitute in a Berlin square in the
summer of 1919. The demobilization of nearly three
million troops in 1918 had accompanied a total
breakdown of industry and the start of rampant
inflation.

Germany, and notably Munich, was rent by conflicting
political ideas inspired by hatred, anger and violence in the
postwar years of the Weimar Republic. In 1918–19 some
300,000 officers, several hundred thousand non-com-
missioned officers and more than two million men were
all too quickly demobilized and thrown on to an empty
labour market. They drifted about Berlin, Munich and
the other big cities, looking for jobs and work, enlisting in
the numerous legalized quasi-military groups, like the
Freikorps, the German People's Offensive and Defensive
Association, the *Stalhelm*, the Home Guard, and Captain
Erhardt's murderous Consul Organization, a group of
political assassins.

Insurrections of both Left and Right were frequent.
They culminated in the Kapp putsch in March 1920, the
overthrow of Bavaria's Socialist Hoffmann Government
and its replacement by Gustav von Kahr's Rightist
dictatorship. Germans were trying desperately to shore
up the ruins of the society they knew, or else conspiring
to impose a new social system more in keeping with their
various aspirations. The social structure was shifting,
breaking up, splitting into armed camps.

It was against this background of social desperation,
economic ruin and the threat of violent revolution that
what Hitler later called 'the miracle' of the rise of Nazism
began.

The first public meeting of Anton Drexler's German
Workers' Party took place in Munich's Hofbräuhaus on 16
October 1919, before an audience of a mere hundred people.
With a rousing defence of German nationalism, Hitler
routed a Bavarian separatist and made the small meeting
a memorable occasion. During the next few weeks the
Party's committee tangled behind the scenes over Drexler's
'25-point programme' and a new name for the Party.

On 24 February 1920, again at the Hofbräuhaus, Hitler,
as propaganda chief, told a cheering audience of about 200
that the Party was now to be called the National Socialist
German Workers' Party (*Nationalsozialistiche Deutsche
Arbeiter Partei*). After a sharp attack on the failings of the
'Weimar Government of traitors', he announced its programme. It demanded abrogation of the Treaty of Versailles, the creation of a new national army, colonies for
Germany, the unity of all German peoples in one European
state, strong anti-Jewish measures, abolition of unearned
incomes, agrarian reform, prohibition of land speculation,
control of the Press and a strong centralized State
authority. The Socialist measures were later dropped, and
a sharp anti-Marxist tone emerged.

From the originally small group attended by members only, Hitler had now created a political party active in the public arena, with an appealing programme and a name holding strongly patriotic overtones. His magnetic oratory, based always on explosive themes, increased his audiences at every meeting. It put the seal of finality on his domination, though not yet his control of the Party. At the same time the speech-making, sometimes at three or four meetings throughout Munich in one evening, taught him lessons in the art of influencing masses of people – the fundamentals of propaganda – that became the foundation of his power. Soon it was clear that no other German political party could vie in this field with the Nazis.

Among the army officers who had joined them at this time was Captain Ernst Röhm, Chief of Staff to the Commandant of the Munich military region and successor to Captain Mayr as chief of Press and Propaganda for the Bavaria Reichswehr group. Röhm, a big, tough, war-scarred professional soldier and a homosexual, with a talent for organization, was concerned only with renewing Germany's greatness, which for him meant military greatness. 'I see the world from the soldier's viewpoint,' he said. But he was also something of a revolutionary. 'We've got to produce something new. A new discipline. A new principle of organization. ... You won't make a revolutionary army out of the old Prussian N.C.O.s.'

Röhm's hopes for toppling the Republican Government were based in part on the Bavarian Home Guard which, in defiance of the Treaty of Versailles, he had built up with hidden arms caches. But early in 1921 the Berlin Government took steps to disband this and some other Bavarian quasi-military groups. Always an opportunist, Röhm at once looked round for an alternative: he saw it in the Nazi Party, and in Hitler especially.

Once he had taken the decision to ride to power on the backs of Hitler and the Nazis, Röhm was a decisive force in the Party's growth. His plan was not merely to help Hitler, whom he saw as an army corporal with a fabulous gift for oratory and a rare insight into propaganda. He planned to control the Party through its projected private army and eventually to seize power for himself. It was the start of a drama of conflict and friendship which ended with Röhm's murder.

Röhm began by injecting into the Party numerous ex-officers upon whom he could rely. At the same time he introduced Hitler to influential people ready to help with funds, or in other ways. Among these were the famed General Erich Ludendorff, and General Ritter von Epp, the Commandant of the Munich military region.

Some of these social introductions seem to have been an ordeal for Hitler. He had not yet rid himself of his social awkwardness despite his ability to orchestrate crowds with his oratory. Otto Strasser, a journalist and Socialist who joined the Party and then broke with Hitler on ideological grounds, tells of a meeting with General Ludendorff and his brother Gregor Strasser. Hitler persistently called Ludendorff 'Excellency', in a half-curt, half-obsequious tone, perching himself awkwardly on the edge of his chair and eventually only breaking his silence with a frenzied attack on Jews.

But once it was known that the Army took a favourable view of the new Nazi Party, a little financial help began to come in. A newspaper was needed to spread Party policy and to print Hitler's speeches. Röhm persuaded General von Epp to raise the 60,000 marks needed to buy the *Völkischer Beobachter*, a weekly at first edited by Dietrich Eckart, which later, under Dr Goebbels, became the most powerful daily in Germany.

Naturally the Party made enemies, and to counter them Hitler raised strong-arm squads, both for protection and for the intimidation by violence in which he so profoundly believed. 'Blind discipline' was the keynote at Nazi meetings, he boasted. 'Anyone who dared to utter so much as a single note of interruption would be mercilessly thrown out ...' From the start, the tone was severely authoritarian. The audience was there to be dictated to and to keep its mouth shut.

The first strong-arm squad, about a dozen men led by a watchmaker, Emil Maurice, who later became Hitler's

Captain (later Major) Ernst Röhm, Chief of Staff to General von Epp in Munich, was invaluable to Hitler as a go-between, winning the support of the Reichswehr generals. He also fashioned the Stormtrooper units into an instrument of violence and terror.

chauffeur, terrorized the Munich Hofbräuhaus gatherings from the 24 February 1920 meeting onwards. A few months later an ex-naval officer, Lieutenant Otto Klintzsch, took over. But Röhm insisted that the force should be properly trained by army officers and be under his command. He enrolled about a hundred tough heavyweights of the 19th Trench Mortar Company, under Captain Streck, to reinforce Hitler's men—'a combat group determined to go to any length', in Hitler's words. They were armed with rubber truncheons and pistols.

Satisfaction grew in him at their violent methods. 'Like a swarm of locusts they swooped down on the disturbers of our meetings, without regard for their superior power ... without regard for wounds and bloody victims...'

In the seething political climate of the day, the very manner of announcement of the meetings—huge red placards with a short inflammatory article in black letters—was a provocation, an invitation to violence by hostile or rival parties, and brawling and violence became customary.

Some of the older Party members, including Anton Drexler, the founder, and Karl Harrer, objected both to Hitler's methods and to Hitler personally, but a majority realized that the Party would be lifeless without Hitler's tireless activity. A clash came, the committee was eventually voted out and on 29 July 1921 Hitler became president, backed by new rules that gave him dictatorial powers. To strengthen his position, he made his army friend Max Amman business manager. From then on Drexler and Harrer faded out.

For the Nazis, and for Hitler, it was a turning point, but they were still weak enough to be swept away by bigger political opponents.

That year the Party held a series of meetings to protest at the vast German reparations payments of 132 million gold marks (£6,600 million) announced in the Paris Agreement. Hitler decided to try to fill the huge Circus building in Munich for this occasion. Lorries swathed in red bunting drove furiously through the city, carrying young Party thugs roaring out Party slogans and scattering leaflets announcing the biggest meeting ever.

The great hall was filled to its 6,000 capacity on three occasions and each time Hitler spoke for over two hours. 'We had for the first time far overstepped the bounds of an ordinary party of the day. We could no longer be ignored,' he recalled later. To mark the event, Hermann Esser, another Nazi speaker, coined the expression Der Führer (the Leader) for Hitler, and it stuck.

Increases both in members, and in enemies among the Leftist Social Democrats and the Communists, followed. Militants among the Left felt that the time to crush the mushrooming Nazi movement had come. They chose a Nazi meeting in the *Festsaal* of the Hofbräuhaus at 7.45 p.m. on 4 November 1921. Hitler learned at the last moment that numbers of Communist workers had been detailed to attend to put as many Nazis as possible permanently out of action.

Only 46 of his strong-arm men were available that night. Hitler solemnly warned them in the vestibule before his speech that they were not to leave the hall unless carried out unconscious or dead. Then he entered the hall surrounded by his bodyguard. During his speech someone in the audience suddenly shouted the Social Democrat slogan, 'Freiheit!' (Freedom). It was the signal.

'In a few moments', Hitler noted in *Mein Kampf*, 'the hall was filled with a yelling and shrieking mob. Beer mugs flew like howitzer shells over their heads. Amid this uproar one heard the cracking of chair legs, the crashing of mugs, bawling, howling and screaming ...

'The dance had not yet begun when my Stormtroopers —for so they were called from this day on—attacked. Like wolves they flung themselves in packs of eight or ten again and again on their enemies, and little by little

Opposite, top: Hitler, accompanied by Julius Streicher, attends a meeting of German nationalist leaders and a march-past of war veterans on 2 September 1920.

Opposite, bottom: Hitler's Headquarters Guard, forerunners of the *Leibstandarte-S.S. Adolf Hitler* (Adolf Hitler Lifeguard), parades before Prince Rupprecht of Bavaria (second left) a few days before the Munich beer-cellar putsch.

actually began to thrash them out of the hall. After five minutes I hardly saw one of them who was not covered with blood . . .

'Then two pistol shots rang out . . . and now a wild din of shooting broke out from all sides. One's heart almost rejoiced at this spectacle, which recalled memories of the War . . . My boys renewed the attack with increased fury, until finally the last disturbers were overcome and flung out of the hall.'

This, and the entire Nazi upsurge of unlimited violence, Hitler himself engineered. An unquenchable thirst for bloodletting possessed him, though not, of course, for sharing personally in the action and risking his own blood. He kept both feet firmly on the touchlines when the brawling began, surrounded by his bodyguard, leaving others to suffer smashed faces and broken bones.

Violence in this context, extending from public meetings to concentration camps, and finally to the violence of actual warfare, was entirely Hitlerian in its development. Encouragement of it was as much part of Hitler's nature as were his vegetarianism and teetotalism.

In the political arena he used violence as an offensive weapon to break up the meetings of other parties, whatever their nature. In his first public avowal of despotism, according to the *Völkischer Beobachter*, he told an audience at the Munich Kindl Keller in 1921 that 'the National Socialist movement in Munich will in future ruthlessly prevent if necessary by force all meetings or lectures that are likely to distract the minds of our fellow citizens . . .'

Any meeting or lecture which incurred his displeasure was henceforward to be the object of an attack by his Stormtroopers. But even Hitler and the Nazis, known as the 'spoilt darlings' of the Bavarian Government, could still go too far. Late in 1921 he ordered the Stormtroopers to rush the platform at a meeting of the separatist Bavarian Association. A brawl followed and the meeting came to an abrupt ending. But its organizer, Herr Ballerstedt, had friends in high places, and, evidently as a severe warning to lay off favoured groups, Hitler was sentenced to three months' imprisonment (though he only served one month) in June 1922.

During this temporary and not uncomfortable deprivation of liberty, Hitler and the Nazis had the chance to reflect on the extraordinary progress they had made during the past year. Though up till April 1921 only an army corporal, he now headed a party which, with about 4,000 members, was still small yet which had made itself a force to be reckoned with in Bavaria. More surprisingly

still, Hitler and the Party now owned a newspaper, with a voice that was constantly gaining in strength.

This success largely came from Hitler and his gifts as orator, propagandist and politician, combined with the demonic energy he directed towards securing his objectives. 'The whole man was passionately devoted to political tactics, with a passion that compelled success', noted the journalist and political editor Rudolf Olden, who was able to observe him closely.

Hitler brandishes his fist in a speech frenzy at a Nazi Youth rally in the '30s.

Hitler's political speeches were totally unlike anything of the kind ever heard before in Germany. They were aimed not at educated people, for whom he professed contempt, but at the German masses, especially the lower middle classes, whose reaction he knew would be one of instinctive approval rather than criticism. The speeches lasted as long as a full-length film or stage play, usually about two and a half hours. Hitler needed time to attain the hypnotic paroxysm which made him master of his listeners thereafter—master of most of those, that is, who were not repelled or disgusted. Olden described his way of speaking as 'an elemental phenomenon, one of nature's marvels':

'It is a falling torrent, a phenomenon such as Nature, in all Creation, has never before produced. . . . He gives the impression of teeming abundance, of a crater that can belch forth all the lava of words that the Earth will hold . . .

'Sooner or later, the moment will come when the speaker is overcome by his own inspiration, and with a sobbing, screaming and gurgling, something unknown and undefinable breaks out of him: it is then no longer a question of set sentences or articulate words—in an ecstasy he speaks "in tongues". Should a man have

remained unmoved up to this stage, now is the time when he becomes aware that before his very eyes there is occurring a manifestation of the unconscious; sense and nonsense have become one, and he finds himself in the presence of an ineffable force of Nature.'

This is the climactic moment towards which the past two and a half hours have been inexorably leading. The sheep in his audience now separate themselves in spirit from the goats, or, as Olden said: 'Those he cannot hypnotize go away nauseated, and never return. The others are his, body and soul. For them he is the redeemer, the national saviour.'

How Hitler sensed the moods of his audiences is described vividly by the journalist Otto Strasser, valuable as a critical observer of Hitler in the early days: 'Adolf Hitler enters a hall. He sniffs the air. For a minute he gropes, feels his way, senses the atmosphere . . .

'His words go like an arrow to their target, he touches each private wound on the raw, liberating the mass unconscious, expressing its innermost aspirations, telling it what it most wants to hear.'

Hitler's ideas about people and what moved them inspired Nazi policy and action. Strasser recorded a statement that explains much of Hitler's entire life. 'Man is congenitally evil,' Hitler told him. 'He can only be controlled by force. To govern him everything is permissible. You must lie, betray, even kill when policy demands it.' He added that this morality was 'only valid for men born to command. It gives them the right to act as masters.'

It was this 'morality' with which Hitler imbued the Stormtroopers and the men he was now beginning to attract to him and offer jobs as functionaries in the growing Nazi Party. When it grew strong enough to dominate the nation, the pursuit of evil, both as a means to an end and simply for its own sake, would largely motivate the Party's activity.

It was in the early 1920s that this and other ideas about controlling people were taking shape in Hitler's mind. One of them concerned the form that political propaganda should take. 'The psyche of the broad masses is accessible only to what is strong and uncompromising . . .' he wrote in *Mein Kampf*. 'They feel very little shame at being terrorized intellectually and they are scarcely conscious of the fact that their freedom as human beings is being impudently abused . . . They see only the ruthless force and brutality of its determined utterances, to which they always submit . . .

'I also came to understand that physical intimidation has its significance for the mass as well as for the individual . . . Intimidation in workshops and in factories, in assembly halls and at mass demonstrations, will always meet with success as long as it does not have to encounter the same kind of terror in a stronger form . . .'

Hitler extolled the power of the Big Lie. In it 'there is always a certain force of credibility . . . The broad masses of a nation . . . more readily fall victims to the big lie than the small lie, since they themselves often tell lies in little matters but would be ashamed to resort to large-scale falsehoods. It would never come into their heads to fabricate colossal untruths and they would not believe that others could have the impudence to distort the truth so infamously.'

Like the I.R.A. today, Hitler discovered, as his Stormtroopers lashed about them and the injuries they wrought were magnified in the public mind, that violence has a propaganda value of its own. He learned that terror as propaganda focuses discussion around its source, repelling many, but riveting the attention of others.

But the terror had to be open and clearly attributable to the Nazis, so the S.A. were put into uniform. A Party member bought up a bargain lot of thousands of brown bush shirts, originally destined for General Paul von Lettow-Vorbeck's troops in German East Africa before the British defeated them in November 1917. The brown shirt eventually became the S.A. uniform, even though Hitler's artistic sensibilities were said to be offended by the colour.

Swastika armbands were already S.A. emblems; Hitler had chosen the female form of this ancient emblem—a cross with equal-sized arms bent at right angles to the right, instead of to the left, as in the male form of the swastika. The rightwards form of this 'Aryan' emblem reputedly symbolizes violence and evil. Hitler apparently chose it on the advice of General Professor Karl Haushofer, a mystic and geopolitical expert, who, aided by Dietrich Eckart, gave Hitler instruction in race theory, occultism and magic rituals.

Hitler himself planned the design of the Nazi flag and standard—a red background with a white disc in its centre bearing the black swastika. 'Not a soul had seen this flag before,' he noted. 'Its effect at that time was something akin to a blazing torch ... The steadily increasing strength of our hall guards was a main factor in popularizing the symbol ... The red expressed the social (not socialist) thought underlying the movement. White the national thought. And the swastika signified the mission allotted to us—the struggle for the victory of Aryan mankind ...'

By early 1922 Nazi Party membership had grown to 6,000. Among the newcomers were one or two who became its luminaries. The notoriously anti-Semitic Julius Streicher, the former leader of the German Socialist Party, had tried to seize the Nazi leadership for himself in Hitler's absence, but had failed, had been forgiven and was lured instead with his Socialists into the Nazi fold. A schoolmaster and avid pornographer, who often carried a long, thick whip in public, Streicher founded *Der Stürmer*, the S.A. newspaper which specialized in scandalous anti-Jewish stories. He became one of Hitler's most loyal followers.

Hermann Goering, the wartime fighter ace, then a lively cosmopolitan personality, who sought excitement and an extreme solution to Germany's vexing problems, was another. Hitler gave him command of the S.A.—officially called the 'Sports and Gymnastic Section'. The proclamation announcing the Section's formation had said that it 'is intended to serve as a means for bringing our youthful members together in a powerful organization for the purpose of utilizing their strength as an offensive force ... to provide a protection for the work of enlightenment about to be accomplished by the leaders. This organization is intended to implant an unrestricted will to action in the hearts of our young followers ...'

Goering, who soon showed an exceptional talent for the techniques of civil disorder, had scant patience with the sport and gymnastic cloak for the S.A.'s true purpose.

Hermann Goering, in Stormtrooper's cap, marching alongside General Ludendorff in Munich on 25 January 1923. Goering was then in command of the S.A.

Perhaps at Röhm's bidding, he set up a headquarters with a staff and commanders for S.A. infantry, artillery, weapons, transport and supply. Reichswehr officers drilled the men and gave them weapons training. This, together with the blood-red swastika standards, gave new glamour to the organization. Soon its membership reached 10,000, with recruits sent in by Röhm from the *Stahlhelm*, the *Reichsbanner* and other para-military groups.

But in this militarization of the Nazis, Hitler lost control of the S.A. to Röhm and the Reichswehr generals. A bitter conflict arose between the two friends, the core of it being a three-way struggle between Hitler on the one hand and Röhm and the Reichswehr generals on the other, over the use to which this very valuable but illegal army should be put.

Hitler regarded the S.A. solely as a political force for strengthening the Party power, ready for action in a coup against the Governments of Bavaria and the Reich—a possibility, he later confessed, that was never out of his thoughts at that time. For the generals the S.A. was a secret military formation with its due place in the Reichswehr's battle order in the war they were contemplating against France. Röhm, as a serving officer and the Reichswehr's link with the Nazis, formally went along with the

REICHSBANKNOTE

HUNDERT
BILLIONEN MARK

WER BANKNOTEN NACHMACHT ODER VERFÄLSCHT ODER NACH-
GEMACHTE ODER VERFÄLSCHTE SICH VERSCHAFFT UND IN VERKEHR
BRINGT, WIRD MIT ZUCHTHAUS NICHT UNTER ZWEI JAHREN BESTRAFT

General Otto von Lossow, C.-in-C. Bavaria, leaves his
Munich home to drive to Army Headquarters.
He realized early in 1923 that Hitler was bent on the
seizure of personal power in Bavaria.

Reichswehr plans, but secretly conspired to use the S.A. for a putsch against both the Bavarian and the Reich Governments in which he would emerge as the dictator.

'Down with France!' the generals muttered in secret. 'Down with the old fogies in the Bavarian and Berlin Governments,' Röhm whispered to his fellow conspirators. 'Not down with France – down with the November criminals,' shouted Hitler at the top of his voice – for he saw that the seizure of power must come before war with France.

In 1922 the terrifying shadow of violent inflation darkened the country. Standing at four to the U.S. dollar at the end of the War, the mark fell to 190 to the dollar by December 1921; 17,900 to the dollar by 31 December 1922; and an incredible 4,200 million to the dollar by November 1923. Misery and despair stalked Germany.

The Government failed to pay reparations. France responded on 11 January 1923 by marching in troops to occupy the Ruhr industrial region and seizing its output of coal and iron. Germany's economic life ground to a near

Opposite, top: This hundred billion mark note bears grim witness to the inflation which gripped Germany by the summer of 1923.

Opposite, bottom: In January 1923, after Germany had defaulted on payment of war reparations, France occupied the industrial region of the Ruhr. Here a French soldier challenges an elderly German.

standstill. Fury swept the country, and, with the Government's backing, a campaign of strikes and sabotage in the Ruhr began, supported by guerilla attacks on French troops. Total ruin faced not the landowning classes, or the peasants, or the factory workers, who had little to lose, but the middle classes – shopkeepers, pensioners, small tradesmen, doctors and lawyers.

France was as much a target of hatred for the Nazis as for anyone now, but Hitler did not lose sight of the main objective – the overthrow of the Government in Berlin. He shouted ever more loudly that the guilty were the 'swindlers of the Jewish stock-exchange conspiracy', though Jewish middle-class families were ruined as completely as non-Jewish ones. But a scapegoat was needed, so Hitler's big lie sped to its target and the Nazis grew stronger.

Hitler saw that in this economic crash, in the psychological instability which went with it, and in the clash with France, lay the chances of an extremist political solution by means of the violent overthrow of the Bavarian and Berlin Governments.

In late 1922 he therefore sharply increased the violent tempo of his demonstrations and meetings, in accord with a new virulence in his speeches. 'We do not pardon, we demand vengeance,' he roared at a meeting in September 1922. 'The dishonouring of the nation must cease. For betrayers of the Fatherland and informers, the gallows is the proper place.'

Among the S.A. and the Nazis, emotions rose to fever pitch at these and similar wild threats. Dr Franz Schweyer, Minister of the Interior, who believed profoundly in the virtue of order, thought he saw the drift of Hitler's intentions. He called for him, and warned him that should he dare to use armed force in a putsch the police would certainly fire on the S.A.

Emotionally, Hitler smote his breast and gave the Herr Minister his word of honour never to try to stage a putsch. Schweyer's answer was blunt: 'All respect to your word, but if you continue making speeches such as you have been making, the stream will one day burst loose of its own accord . . .'

The first of a series of crises now flared. Hitler had planned a big Nazi Party conference for 25 January 1923, and S.A. men were flocking into Munich from all over Bavaria. Concerned at the presence of these Sormtroopers, and doubting the value of Hitler's word, Schweyer issued orders forbidding it.

Hitler was now in a quandary. Were he to defy Schweyer and proceed, he faced the likelihood of arrest for himself and a clash between the S.A. and armed units of police and army, which could have only one outcome. On the other hand it would be disastrous for his prestige if he ignominiously sent his men home.

He pleaded with Röhm for help, and Röhm saved the day by appealing to General von Epp, his commanding officer. In turn, von Epp outlined the issue to General Otto von Lossow, a right-wing monarchist and the Reichswehr G.O.C. in Bavaria, who had recently been appointed by the Reichswehr G.O.C., General Hans von

Seeckt, to keep a tight rein on Bavarian extremists and forestall the chance of a putsch.

Von Lossow now sent for Hitler, and, pointing out that if the worst came to the worst the Army would carry out orders to have the S.A. shot down, obtained his promise not to stage a putsch on 26 January. In return he gave permission for the conference to be held. His reason for giving it, he told Schweyer, was that he did not wish to demoralize these valuable nationalist elements.

For Hitler the event was a double victory. He had defeated the Bavarian Government and at the same time had shown that he was under Reichswehr protection. He saw to it that the conference was the most peaceful ever – an orderly presentation of standards to S.A. formations, and a speech in which he forecast that unless 'the betrayers of the German Fatherland' in Berlin were 'done away with' before a new war 'the German Siegfried will again be stabbed in the back.'

Because his speeches usually went unreported – and because the Party needed more publicity, Dietrich Eckart, at Hitler's request, changed the *Völkischer Beobachter* on 8 February 1923 from a weekly to a daily newspaper. Alfred Rosenberg, the architect and writer on racist theory who saw himself as the Nazis' 'chief ideologist', became editor-in-chief. A loan in priceless dollars from friend and supporter Putzi Hanfstaengl enabled Hitler to acquire the paper himself from von Epp's backers, and also to buy a modern rotary press.

It was a step towards making the paper some years later Germany's biggest. Whether at this time the money the Nazis were alleged to be receiving from French sources in return for Hitler's naming the German Government, not France, as enemy number one helped him in acquiring the paper has never been proved.

Meanwhile Röhm, by persuasion and diplomacy, had bound the various quasi-military nationalist groups in Bavaria, including the Nazis, into an alliance named the Working Union of Patriotic Combat Leagues. Ludendorff was its patron and it was militarily under the control of Lieutenant-Colonel Kriebel.

Schweyer, Minister of the Interior, was seriously worried by this development. In Bavaria, the only German state in which the Nazi Party had not been banned (the Reichswehr would not have let Schweyer ban it), political tension had again risen. The expectation of another putsch increased daily, both from the Right and from the Marxists.

The climax came when Hitler and Kriebel planned a mass attack on the Social Democratic and Communist May Day demonstrations by armed formations of the Patriotic Combat Leagues. Urgent orders were distributed throughout Bavaria for members to gather in Munich by 30 April. Hitler asked General von Lossow to supply him for one day with arms and ammunition over and above those they already had, for use against 'the internal

enemy'. He reminded von Lossow of an earlier promise more or less to this effect.

But von Lossow knew that after dealing with the Left, Hitler might try to overthrow the Government in Bavaria, which it was his duty to protect. According to Konrad Heiden, he told Hitler: 'You may call me a rascally perjurer if you like, but I'm not going to hand over the weapons.' And he warned that he would order the Reichswehr into action against any groups who started trouble on 1 May.

Hitler was now in a much worse dilemma than that of January. For not only S.A. troops but also those of Captain Heiss's *Reichsbanner* and Dr Weber's *Oberland Freikorps* were pouring into Munich by the thousand, all

Hitler, flanked by Alfred Rosenberg (left), the Nazi philosopher of race theory, and Dr Franz Weber, leader of the *Oberland Freikorps*, an independent military formation, awaits the right moment to begin a public speech in Munich in late 1922.

of them joyfully believing that they were to take part in the long-expected putsch. It was thought, incorrectly, that Ludendorff himself was involved.

Hitler and Röhm knew that they could not turn back now without making themselves ridiculous. Equally, they needed many more weapons for the intended brush with the Communists. Röhm now in effect mutinied, driving into the Munich infantry barracks with a convoy of lorries and a company of S.A., and bluffing those in charge to let him load all the machine-guns and ammunition he wanted for Hitler and Kriebel.

Not long after dawn next day, 1 May 1923, about 20,000 men of the Patriotic Combat Leagues, mainly S.A., had already assembled, in well-worn field-grey 1914–18

uniforms and steel helmets, on the vast Oberwiesenfeld parade ground in the outer suburbs. Hermann Goering was there at the head of the S.A., in brown shirt, breeches and jack boots, together with Hess, Streicher with his whip, Gregor Strasser and his pale young assistant Heinrich Himmler—'all the big and little actors in the Hitlerian drama,' the journalist Otto Strasser noted, 'those destined to play leading roles, those destined to remain in obscurity, those destined to be ruthlessly obliterated.'

They were waiting for the expected message from Röhm that the Communists were on the march and that the time had come for them to enter the city and attack. The hours passed slowly in the hot sun and still Röhm's message failed to come. Hitler began to fear treachery.

At about midday the worst happened. Armed units of the Reichswehr, flanked by green-uniformed armed police, appeared in the distance. Among the officers at their head was the burly figure of Röhm. That morning he had been called before a furious General von Lossow to be severely reprimanded for removing the weapons, and had then been ordered to march with the army and police units, at the risk of a bloody clash with his friends, to retrieve the weapons he had given them and prevent them from entering the city.

Heavily outnumbered, the Government force entered the parade ground and, while Hitler, Kriebel and Goering stood there indecisively, swiftly surrounded them. Röhm and Hitler met in the no-man's-land between the two forces. Otto Strasser noted that Hitler's eyes were flashing and that he seemed almost to be foaming at the mouth. 'Have you betrayed us?' Strasser heard him shout.

Röhm answered coldly, according to Strasser: 'The time is not yet ripe. The Government and the Reichswehr are tolerating the Red First of May demonstrations.'

Peace or civil war in Bavaria now hung at this moment on a delicate thread. Hitler stalked back to his officers and repeated that the time was not yet ripe. Kriebel and Gregor Strasser refused abject surrender and demanded that with their superior forces they accept the Reichswehr challenge, fire upon and overpower the heavily outnumbered Government units, and march into Munich.

The crunch had come, but Hitler had lost his nerve. Despite an argument that went on for hours, he refused. Eventually the arms were given up and returned to the barracks. Ignominiously, the men dispersed and assembled in the Krone Circus area, where Hitler in a rousing speech bitterly condemned the 'November criminals'. 'The humiliating memory of the Oberwiesenfeld defeat was never effaced from Hitler's mind,' Otto Strasser noted later. 'The rancour he nourished against Röhm was born that day.'

But Hitler still believed that the vacillating Bavarian Government could be overthrown by swift action and ruthless force. Events throughout Germany, no less than his impatience, were to usher in before the year's end the ambitious blow called the 'beer-cellar putsch'.

Overleaf: A smiling Hitler doffs his hat as he leaves a Party meeting in a Munich beer cellar in 1925.

PROPAGANDA
'The Big Lie'

Above: A still from Leni Riefenstahl's film of the Munich Olympics of 1936.

Right: Leni Riefenstahl, whose *Triumph of the Will*, a record of the Nuremberg Rally of 1934, was a paean to Hitler and a masterpiece of lyrical propaganda.

Propaganda, and violence—these were the mainsprings of the rise to power of Hitler and the Nazi Party. Hitler believed profoundly in the political effectiveness of both. In the years of beer-hall speeches and fights by his Stormtroopers, he had learned by experience what they could be expected to achieve: how violence, or the daily threat of it, could create a fear psychosis in the great masses of the people, thus intensifying the effect of propaganda. Simplicity in propaganda was therefore imperative. 'All effective propaganda,' he declared, 'must be confined to a few bare necessities and then must be expressed in a few stereotyped formulas.'

Barefaced lies were also a necessity, part of the stuff of Nazi politics, but the lie had to be big. 'In the big lie there is always a certain force of credibility . . . The grossly impudent lie always leaves traces behind it, even if it has been nailed down,' Hitler wrote.

Hitler believed, and put this belief into effect, that propaganda was as much a part of war as artillery, and could be used as a psychological weapon to soften up the enemy both before and during hostilities. 'The place of artillery preparation for frontal attack will in future be taken by

revolutionary propaganda before the armies begin to function . . .' he declared, in an exaggeration which nevertheless held a kernel of truth. 'How to achieve the moral breakdown of the enemy before the war has started—that is the problem.' Certainly French morale and will to resist were lowered in the late 1930s by the brilliant and incessant propaganda about the invincibility of Germany's new army.

During the war, when Hitler was preoccupied with military affairs, Dr Goebbels was in entire charge of propaganda. His policy, to which he adhered scrupulously, aimed to undermine the Allies' will to resist, to create a split between Allied governments and their peoples, and to instil in the German people a belief in their ultimate victory.

Like Hitler he insisted on simplification, primitive arguments, endless repetition of slogans and lies; the publication of news reports in the form of commentaries, so as to avoid objectivity; and disregard of war aims and of the future except for the certainty of victory. The whole of Germany's press and radio output was dominated by these propaganda values.

Above: A scene from *Triumph of the Will.*

Below: A scene from the film *Jüd Süss*, in which Nazi anti-Semitism gave a twisted view of eighteenth-century history.

Above: A montage from *Hitlerjunge Quex* (1933), a film which pitted a Nazi son against a Communist father.

The Beer-Cellar Putsch

Gustav von Kahr, the extreme right-wing Premier of Bavaria in 1923, opposed both the Weimar Republic and the Nazi bid for power; he was already plotting to restore the Bavarian Monarchy.

Opposite page: Colonel-General Hans von Seeckt (left), C.-in-C. of the new German Army in 1923, discusses the threat of a Nazi putsch in Munich with his aide, Lieutenant Hasse. Von Seeckt defended the Weimar Republic against threats from both Left and Right.

Hitler and Röhm realized independently that events might now present them with a rare opportunity for seizing power. Wilhelm Cuno's Reich Government fell with the total collapse of the mark. Gustav Stresemann, leader of the right-wing German People's Party, formed a coalition Government with the Social Democrats, and on 26 September 1923 ended the costly passive resistance in the Ruhr with a policy of reconciliation with France and of cooperation with the West.

Nazis and Communists alike opposed him strongly — both were hostile to the Republic and to parliamentary democracy. Hitler, who since his May Day fiasco had been living in the mountains near Berchtesgaden, watching, and meditating the chances of another putsch, appeared again in Munich and began a campaign denouncing Stresemann's policy as a 'betrayal', openly demanding an uprising. Echoing Mussolini's Fascist March on Rome of the previous year, he called for a 'march on Berlin'.

On 25 September 1923, the day after Stresemann had ended the so-called 'Ruhr War', the leaders and associates of the Union of Combat Leagues met in Munich at Röhm's call to discuss their immediate policy, including mobilization plans. Hitler strode on to the stage and in an impassioned two-hour speech pleaded to be made the Union's

political chief. It was to be remembered because it brought tears to the eyes of the sensitive Hess and made even the war-scarred Röhm weep openly. Hitler was elected, chief now of a force estimated at 25,000 including the 15,000-strong S.A., though Ludendorff remained its front man.

The Bavarian Government reacted nervously. The very next day its leader, Freiherr von Knilling, proclaimed a state of emergency which included the suspension of civil rights, the imposition of martial law and the appointment of Gustav Ritter von Kahr, the right-wing monarchist, as State Commissioner with dictatorial powers.

The event had repercussions on all sides. Fearing a move towards Bavarian separatism, an attempt to restore the monarchy, or a Hitler putsch, President Ebert decreed a nationwide state of emergency the same day, with martial law. In effect this made Reichswehr G.O.C. General von Seeckt the most powerful man in Germany and increased Hitler's growing apprehension, for he was aware that von Seeckt was watching him. And since General von Lossow, G.O.C. in Bavaria, had agreed to support von Kahr in a putsch aimed at restoring the Bavarian monarchy in the person of Prince Rupprecht, he knew he could not count on any help from von Lossow's troops.

On September 30, von Seeckt gave unmistakable

evidence of his opinion of putschists by sending troops to crush an uprising near Berlin by the so-called Black Reichswehr, a secret military organization. Its leader, Major Ernst Buchrucker, was sentenced to 10 years' imprisonment. At the end of October von Seeckt also moved to suppress the Red militia in Saxony, and ordered the arrest of Communist and Socialist deputies. Communists in Hamburg and Thuringia also felt the weight of his authority.

Von Seeckt's efforts to bring Bavaria under control were like a game of chess fought between him and President Ebert against von Kahr, von Lossow, Hitler and Ludendorff. Probably at von Seeckt's suggestion, Field-Marshal von Hindenburg telegraphed a warning to Ludendorff—which was made public—against involving himself with any projected putsch. Far from pouring oil on troubled waters, it inflamed Ludendorff and Hitler to the extent that they announced an impending march on Berlin, and at the same time launched a virulent attack in the *Völkischer Beobachter* on von Seeckt and President Ebert. Not to be outdone, von Kahr, as State Commissioner, proclaimed Bavaria's independence of the Reich Government. He then refused Ebert's demand for a ban on the newspaper, while von Lossow spurned von Seeckt's order to arrest the nationalist agitators.

It was Ebert's move now, and, with von Seeckt's consent, on 23 October 1923 he dismissed von Lossow as Reichswehr G.O.C. in Bavaria and replaced him with General Kress von Kressenstein. Von Kahr countered this in his capacity as State Commissioner by appointing von Lossow as G.O.C. Reichswehr troops in Bavaria, which, though sounding the same, was an inferior post. Von Seeckt's answer was to issue an order reminding the Bavarian troops of their loyalty oath.

Meanwhile, on 16 October 1923, Kriebel, in agreement with Hitler and Ludendorff, brought civil war a step nearer with the order for the stand-by mobilization of the troops of the Combat Leagues. The word went round among them that the anticipated march on Berlin was timed for 15 November, but there was little real unity among the putschists.

On 23 October, Goering discussed the intended putsch against Berlin with S.A. leaders and told them: 'Anyone who makes the least difficulty is to be shot. Leaders must find out right away the personalities who must be removed.' Goering and Kriebel believed that Ludendorff would emerge as dictator when the smoke had cleared. 'There is no question of a leading position for Hitler,' Kriebel was telling German observers from the north—though Hitler saw himself as Germany's saviour. 'Ludendorff's function will be purely military,' he told one of von Lossow's staff. 'I need him in order to win over the Reichswehr. He will have no say whatever in politics.' Thus there was conflict both between Munich and Berlin and between the various

putschists in Munich themselves, all of whom wanted something different.

Hitler had tried during many talks to win over von Lossow to the side of the Nazis and the Combat Leagues. 'A military leader who revolts against his chief,' he remarked grimly, 'must be determined either to go to extremes or to be struck down as an ordinary mutineer and rebel.'

But von Lossow and Colonel Hans von Seisser, the Bavarian police chief, were firmly committed to the monarchist putsch von Kahr was planning in his rather uncertain way. Von Kahr had no intention of getting in the same boat with Hitler and his bloodthirsty revolutionaries, not even when Ludendorff himself tried to persuade him. He was ready, but cautious. 'I will march, but only when there is a 51 per cent chance of success,' he was quoted as saying.

Between the two sides, events came to a head on 7 November; Kriebel declared openly that cooperation was impossible between them and threw down the gauntlet. Hitler, Röhm, Kriebel, Goering and the Combat League troops were now free, if they dared, to make a bid for power in Munich as a prelude to the march on Berlin.

At first they planned to mobilize all their forces for manœuvres on a heath just outside Munich on 11–12 November and seize power then. But on 7 November Hitler received news from Max von Scheubner-Richter, one of his political advisers, that von Kahr might possibly anticipate him and move first on 12 November. Unlikely as this was, he nevertheless decided to disregard all the earlier detailed planning—to act at once, with the few hundred S.A. he could mobilize.

A meeting on 8 November called by von Kahr, von Lossow and von Seisser, which would be attended by the Bavarian military and civil establishment, monarchists especially, at the Bürgerbräu Cellar, was to lead opinion and be the curtain-raiser for the von Kahr putsch.

Hitler persuaded Röhm and Kriebel that they must disregard their earlier plans, act now and seize power first. Von Kahr's meeting was to be the occasion for the seizure, and by an incredible piece of bluff he and his two associates were to be tricked or compelled into joining forces with them. Kriebel accordingly send orders to the Combat Leagues to mobilize in Munich at once.

There was little time. Barely 600 armed S.A. Stormtroopers were ready in Munich by midday on 8 November, though Gregor Strasser was expected later with 350 men from Landshut. Max von Scheubner-Richter was sent hurriedly by car to bring Ludendorff, who had not been told of the new plan, from his villa at Ludwigshöhe, an outer suburb of Munich.

Hitler, juggling airily with Germany's future that morning, already saw himself as dictator of the Reich. He wore a frockcoat for the occasion, pinned his Iron Cross on it and put a loaded revolver in his pocket. The meeting in the smart Bürgerbräu Cellar, a spacious rendezvous in Munich's eastern suburbs on the south bank of the Isar river, had begun at about 8 p.m. Von Kahr, gazing out across the smoke-filled hall, where the 3,000 Bavarian notables sat at tables with their beermugs, was droning on through a a speech against Marxism, with von Lossow and von Seisser flanking him on the platform.

Suddenly, at 8.30, the doors were flung open and, headed by Goering, a squad of Stormtroopers in steel helmets, armed with rifles and revolvers, burst in and, overturning tables and upsetting beermugs, forced their way towards the platform. Hitler, among the leading group, jumped up on to a table and silenced the din with two shots from his revolver into the ceiling. In a hoarse and excited voice he shouted:

'The national revolution has begun! The cellar is sur-

rounded by 600 armed men. No one may leave. The Bavarian Government has been overthrown and a provisional Reich Government formed. The Reichswehr and the police barracks have been seized. Troops and police are marching under the swastika.'

For a moment there was a shocked silence, then a loud stir filled the great hall. Hitler kept the action going and, ascending the stage, motioned with his revolver for von Kahr, von Lossow and von Seisser to go into an adjoining room with him.

There are various accounts of what followed. The most dramatic has it that Hitler produced his revolver and

pointed it at his own head, with the words: 'Gentlemen, if I should fail, not one of us shall leave this room alive. There are three of you and I have four bullets'.

He then declared himself to be chief of a new Reich Government; Ludendorff, G.O.C. of the new Reichswehr, soon to march on Berlin; von Lossow, Defence Minister; and von Seisser, Reich Police Minister. In Bavaria he had appointed State Police President Pöhner Minister President with full powers and von Kahr State Regent.

Meanwhile, angry noises were arising from the notables in the main hall, where Goering had taken over. In a menacing voice Goering told them that a new Government was now being appointed next door, adding contemptuously: 'For that matter, you've got nothing to grumble about. You've got your beer!'

At that moment, Hitler rushed back on to the stage and shouted in an excited voice that full agreement had been reached about the formation of the provisional German National Government, whose task would be 'to organize the march on that sinful Babel, Berlin . . . Tomorrow will see either a National Government in Germany or the death of us.'

Having tricked his audience into believing that von Kahr and von Lossow were fully in agreement with him, he went

Ernst Pöhner, the police president of Munich until shortly before the Hitler putsch. He aided the Nazis and arranged with his former assistant, Wilhelm Frick, for the police not to intervene when Hitler began his bid for power in the Bürgerbräu Cellar on 8 November 1923.

back into the room. Ludendorff arrived, looking angry at having been left out of the great decision and at being made chief of the Army instead of head of the new Government. But he restrained himself, agreed to collaborate and advised those present to do the same. Hitler added that in any case there was no going back now. 'The event is already world history.' Von Kahr eventually agreed.

The five of them then strode back on to the platform, where at Hitler's request each made a short declaration of support for Hitler's 'national revolution'. Von Kahr spoke ambiguously of his 'heavy heart' and 'the good of our native Bavaria and our great German Fatherland'. In a stage whisper Hitler exclaimed gratefully: 'Excellency, I will stand behind you as faithfully as a dog.'

The State and the Munich police chiefs, Pöhner and von Seisser, expressed suitably colourless sentiments. Ludendorff referred to his surprise at the event and to his being 'profoundly moved by the greatness of the moment'. Hitler declared that he would now fulfil the vow he had made 'as a blind cripple' in military hospital five years ago: 'not to rest until the November criminals were overthrown, until on the ruins of the wretched Germany of today there had

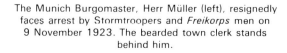

The Munich Burgomaster, Herr Müller (left), resignedly faces arrest by Stormtroopers and *Freikorps* men on 9 November 1923. The bearded town clerk stands behind him.

Bavarian mounted police armed with short lances and rifles disperse pro-Nazi crowds in the Munich Odeonsplatz on 9 November after the gendarmerie had fired on Hitler and his followers.

arisen once more a Germany of power, of greatness, of freedom and splendour'. While the audience stood on the tables and cheered passionately, he then shook hands warmly with each in turn.

Only one discordant note was sounded in this seemingly joyful scene. Minister of the Interior Dr Franz Schweyer stepped up on to the stage, walked boldly up to Hitler, and, wagging his finger like a disapproving magistrate, asked him sternly if he remembered his promise not to carry out a putsch. For Hitler, in this ecstatic moment, it was a forgotten promise, an irrelevance. He made no reply, and Schweyer was led away under arrest. But now, instead of keeping the strictest personal control of the ruling triumvirate of Bavaria, whom he had seemingly overthrown, Hitler carelessly left the Cellar and went to mediate in a clash between troops and S.A. trying to seize the Engineers' barracks.

It was a fatal error. He returned soon after to find von Kahr, von Lossow and von Seisser gone. Ludendorff had accepted their word as German officers that they meant what they had said. Hitler and his Nazis had now lost the initiative, for the trio, furious at the indignities and the duress to which they had been subjected, made swift plans to crush this revolt.

It would not be hard, for, contrary to Hitler's declaration, the Reichswehr and police barracks had not been occupied; nor were troops marching under the swastika. None of the railway stations, city road junctions or telegraph offices had been seized—only the Reichswehr headquarters, where Röhm had set up machine-gun posts and barbed-wire defences. And although some 3,000 S.A. and Combat League men had gathered in the city, General Kress von Kressenstein, urged on by von Seeckt, whom Ebert had made military dictator, was now bringing in reinforcements ready for stern action.

Hitler and Ludendorff raced across the river to the Reichswehr headquarters, to be confronted by hostility where they had expected support. They returned anxiously to the Cellar, awaiting word from von Lossow and von Kahr, but none came, and messengers failed to return. The putsch, it dawned upon them, had failed.

The next morning, Ludendorff took control and told the crestfallen and alarmed Hitler that they would march across the city to relieve Röhm, by now under siege in the Reichswehr headquarters. Ludendorff hoped that on seeing him, their war hero, at the head of the putschists, the troops and police might flock to support them.

The column of some 3,000 S.A. and Combat League

men, joined by officer cadets of the Infantry School, crossed the Ludwig bridge over the Isar, and, headed by Ludendorff in a green felt hat and an old shooting jacket, and Hitler in his trenchcoat, marched, singing, behind the blood-red, limp swastika banners through the damp autumnal streets lined with excited crowds. Upon the walls they saw evidence of von Kahr's swift duplicity—proclamations in heavy black type stating that the declaration forced from him at revolver point was null and void and that the Nazi Party and the Combat Leagues were dissolved.

Marching eight abreast past the National Opera House, they entered the narrow Residenzstrasse leading to the broad Odeonsplatz, on the corner of which towered an imposing building named the Feldherrnhalle, the Hall of the Field-Marshals. On its wide steps were grouped about a hundred of Colonel von Seisser's green-uniformed police, armed with carbines. Unruffled, Ludendorff marched on, with his adjutant Major Streck on one side of him and Hitler, Scheubner-Richter and Kriebel on the other. Goering and Julius Streicher were in the following line. Another of von Seisser's police units now barred their way at the entrance to the Odeonsplatz, evidently determined to stop them in the narrow street where their numbers would count for less.

A command rang out: the police raised their carbines and took aim. Accounts differ as to what happened next. One says that Julius Streicher ran forward shouting to them not to fire, but was thrust aside and knocked down. Another, that Hitler's bodyguard Ulrich Graf ran towards the officer in command with arms outstretched and shouted to the police: 'Don't shoot! It is Excellency Ludendorff and Hitler.'

Ignoring this plea, as Ludendorff led the marchers steadily along the street towards his men, Baron von Godin, the officer in charge of the police, shouted the order to fire and a volley of bullets rang down the street. Some of the foremost Nazis—some reports say Hitler himself—fired back.

When the shooting stopped, sixteen Nazis and three police lay huddled dead on the ground. Hitler, unwounded, fell heavily and dislocated his shoulder, while Scheubner-Richter dropped dead beside him. Goering, just behind, fell badly wounded in the groin. The column scattered. Ludendorff, according to *The Times* reporter, also threw himself to the ground, but quickly got to his feet and marched on through the police cordon and into the Odeonsplatz, where he was deferentially taken into custody. Orders had apparently been given not to fire at him.

After a few seconds Hitler also got up and staggered back down the narrow street. A yellow car nosed its way slowly through the throng and someone shouted for Hitler. Dr Walter Schulz, a Nazi physician, bundled him into it and took him to the Hanfstaengls' villa at Uffing, 37 miles away. Goering was carried into another car and driven across the Austro-German frontier by his wife Karin. Two hours later Röhm surrendered at the Reichswehr headquarters.

Hitler's stupendous confidence trick, which was intended to herald a march on Berlin, had failed little more than a

mile from where it began. But for two days afterwards thousands of Munich's citizens and students demonstrated in support of it, insulted the police and the Reichswehr troops, and labelled von Kahr a traitor. It was useless. The conspirators were now under arrest, or had crossed the frontier into Austria. Hitler's last-minute shuffling of their original plans on 8 November had probably lost the day. He was arrested in his pyjamas in the Hanfstaengls' villa on 11 November.

In February 1924 Hitler, Ludendorff, Röhm, Frick, Pöhner, Kriebel and many other Nazis and putschists stood trial for high treason before a special Munich court. They were accused of trying to overthrow the Bavarian and Reich Governments by force. It was hardly a normal,

Far left: Hitler, clutching his felt hat convulsively and obviously under severe strain, leaves the court in the Munich School of Infantry after receiving his sentence. He is accompanied by Ludendorff, Röhm and Brückner.

Left: Dr Hjalmar Schacht, who was appointed Financial Commissioner with special powers in November 1923, brought German inflation under control and created a stable currency, the Rentenmark, by June 1924.

Below: Ludendorff acknowledges salutes on leaving the court in Munich after his acquittal on a charge of high treason for the attempted overthrow of the Bavarian Government.

straightforward trial. Von Kahr, von Lossow and von Seisser, the main prosecution witnesses, were deeply implicated, while Franz Gürtner, the Minister of Justice and a friend of Hitler, had passed the word to the judges for leniency.

The sentences, on 1 April 1924, were acquittal for Ludendorff, and for Hitler the minimum of five years' detention with a recommendation for a big remission. These were absurdly lenient and shed light on the real climate of political feeling in Munich. 'We must support the National Socialists,' the Minister of Justice said publicly, 'they are flesh of our flesh.'

During the well-reported three-week trial Hitler became famous throughout Germany, with his vivid exposition of his 'patriotic' role and of the Nazi policy for a rejuvenated nation. Röhm was found guilty, but was discharged on the same day; without delay he began to reorganize the forces of the forbidden Combat Leagues into a new, similar organization called the *Frontbann*.

Röhm still believed that his new military section should be purely a fighting organization, represented in the political movement, but not subordinate to it or hindered by it. A prominent Nazi, Kurt Ludecke, aided him by visiting group leaders in cities throughout Germany, Berlin included, to ally them with the Nazis, for Ludecke was impressed by Röhm. 'He was a brilliant leader of men . . . fearless and straightforward. His massive round head, battle-scarred and patched, looked like something hammered from rock. He was the living image of war itself, in contrast to his polished manner and instinctive courtesy. That, with his naturalness, diplomatic tact and *savoir faire* distinguished him from leading Nazis, then and afterwards, who for the most part were boorish and arrogant, or were bullies . . . He was a passionate politician, having, for a soldier, a rare intelligence and understanding of politics.'

Ludecke noted that many of the men he visited on Röhm's behalf 'were veritable *condottieri*, such as Captain von Heydebreck and Edmund Heines. Almost without exception they resumed Röhm's work eagerly, only too glad to be busy again at the secret military work without which they found life wearisome.'

These *condottieri* were raising a terrible sword of Damocles over the heads of the German people, but Hitler wanted a fighting force – so long as it was both independent of the Reichswehr and subordinate to himself. Therefore the resentment he felt towards Röhm for opposing him began inexorably to grow.

Life for Hitler at the fortress of Landsberg, in an attractive part of the Bavarian countryside, was no hardship. He was permitted books and writing materials in his well-furnished room, and quickly he set to work dictating *Mein Kampf*, at first to Ulrich Graf, his bodyguard, and later to Rudolf Hess, who voluntarily joined him there. The food was as good as anything he had ever had, and the company, some forty other Nazis, agreeable. His only worry was the fate of the movement he had created in the power struggles that began to plague it.

In 1924 a radical economic revival began in Germany. Dr Hjalmar Schacht, the so-called financial wizard, stopped

In this Nazi propaganda picture, Hitler is shown
languishing behind bars in the fortress of Landsberg.

Hitler's relatively congenial confinement in Landsberg is reflected in this picture. He is accompanied by Colonel Kriebel, Rudolf Hess (who joined him voluntarily) and Weber. The man with the mandolin is Emil Maurice, Hitler's chauffeur. It was during this period that Hitler wrote much of *Mein Kampf*.

inflation almost overnight with the creation of a new and stable currency, the gold Rentenmark. The American Dawes Plan pared down reparations payments and made foreign investment in the reconstruction of German industry attractive. Germany was lent more money than she was paying out in reparations and, ironically, the Allies were financing their own compensation for war damages. Agreement on the French departure from the Ruhr was won, while the wider political settlement of the Locarno Pact was soon to be achieved. Although older people and some of the middle classes had been ruined and working men's wages stayed appallingly low, prosperity began to flow back.

The Nazi Party, now illegal, changed its name to the National Socialist Freedom Party under the leadership of Alfred Rosenberg, and its candidates—despite Hitler's opposition—took part in the Reichstag spring elections of 1924, winning a surprising 32 seats, with just under two million votes. Gottfried Feder, Wilhelm Frick, Ludendorff, Röhm and Gregor Strasser were among those elected. But quarrels among the leaders so split the Party's unity that as a political force it became ineffectual during this year of German recovery, when rabid nationalism was on the wane.

In the Reichstag December elections its share of seats fell to 14, with less than a million votes. In fact Hitler himself, who in view of police moves to deport him to Austria had resigned his leadership of the Party on 8 July, fostered this disunity so that while he was in prison no rival could emerge and take over. However, reflecting upon the loss of liberty that illegal action had brought him, he was now impressed by the possibilities of winning power by legal, democratic means. 'Instead of working to achieve power by an armed coup we shall have to hold our noses and enter the Reichstag against the Catholic and Marxist deputies,' he told Kurt Ludecke, who visited him at Landsberg. 'Sooner or later we shall have a majority—and after that, Germany. I am convinced this is our best line of action, now that conditions in the country have changed so radically.'

But Hitler's biggest worry was how soon he would be freed, for Röhm's activities had created fresh anxiety in the Bavarian Government, now led by Minister-President Dr Heinrich Held of the Catholic People's Party. This had caused Hitler's release, provisionally fixed for October, to be postponed.

But the Nazis' loss of so many seats in the Reichstag elections persuaded the Government that the Nazis were on the wane. Minister of Justice Franz Gürtner's influence was decisive. A telegram reached Landsberg on 20 December ordering the immediate release of Hitler and Kriebel.

Wearing an old trenchcoat over his leather shorts, Hitler was driven by car back to his flower-bedecked Munich apartment. Almost feverishly, and without any apparent fear of failure, he set to work to re-establish the Nazi Party.

THE RALLIES
Symbol of National Unity

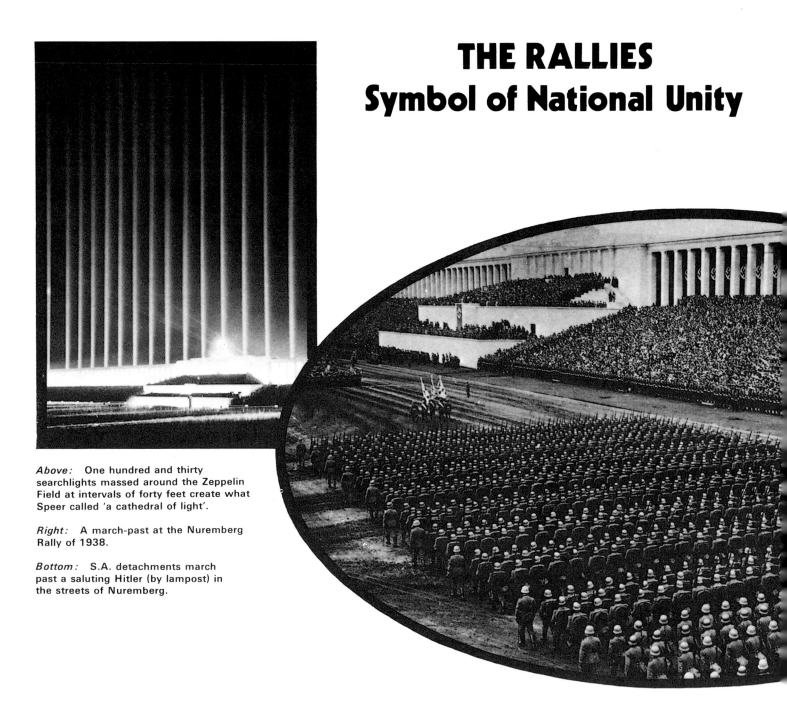

Above: One hundred and thirty searchlights massed around the Zeppelin Field at intervals of forty feet create what Speer called 'a cathedral of light'.

Right: A march-past at the Nuremberg Rally of 1938.

Bottom: S.A. detachments march past a saluting Hitler (by lampost) in the streets of Nuremberg.

High in the night sky the cone of searchlights spread like a cathedral of light. Spotlights in the arena lit up the forest of blood-red banners, the regiments of uniformed men marching in step with the defiant beat of massed bands. Flaming torches added a barbaric note to the tension and excitement of this dramatic pageantry. Suddenly a mighty roar—'Sieg Heil! Sieg Heil!' The Führer was mounting the granite podium.

Nuremberg is the name linked with the mammoth Nazi annual rallies, for all eleven of them except the first (Munich, 1923) and the third (Weimar, 1926) were staged there, while war stopped the twelfth. Hitler chose this ancient Bavarian city, rather than Munich, as their permanent locale because it had become the symbol of the German nationalism of which Nazism saw itself as the inheritor.

A dramatic mixture of a pagan festival in Rome's ancient Colosseum and a superb Wagnerian operatic presentation, these eight-day rallies made German politics tangible and immediate. No man or boy present was a simple spectator.

Everyone was personally involved, because his fate, his destiny, were directly caught up in the breathtaking flow of events, speeches and pageantry.

At Nuremberg Hitler was filled with fresh confidence in his extraordinary powers. In the great arena his voice rose and fell to overawe the nations of Europe; to threaten Austria, Czechoslovakia or Poland. His every word was flashed around the world and he felt himself at one with the German people as the well-drilled Nazi legions cheered and marched like a nation in miniature.

The Nuremberg arena that the Nazis built for the 1936 rally accommodated 400,000 men, with seats for 350,000 spectators in stone grandstands. A vast Congress Hall seated 20,000, and in 1935 work began on another to hold twice as many. Still Hitler was not satisfied. In 1936 he launched work on a grand avenue of triumph paved with granite, 240 feet wide and 16 miles long; then, in 1937, on a sports arena to seat over 300,000 people. Ironically, only war, which the Nuremberg rallies symbolized, stopped this lust to build.

Albert Speer's eagle—over one hundred feet in wing span—dominates the Zeppelin Field.

The Nazis Fight for Power

General Ludendorff greets Nazi members of the
Tannenberg League in 1924. Wilhelm Brückner, who
became Hitler's personal adjutant, stands behind him.

The ban on the Nazis was the main obstacle to be overcome, for little could be done until it had been removed, and the old name of National Socialist German Workers' Party, the blood-red swastika banners and the *Völkischer Beobachter*, the strident anti-Semitic newspaper, were permitted once more. Two weeks after his release, while still on probation, Hitler took the bull by the horns and obtained an interview with Dr Held to propose an alliance between Catholics and Nazis 'to combat Marxism'.

He promised that his new policy of legality and no putsches guaranteed respect for the State's authority, but, of course, nothing could be done unless the Party was allowed to exist again.

Gürtner's influence, combined with Hitler's eloquence, triumphed. With a frosty warning about respect for the law, Held—this worthy, unsuspecting Catholic—agreed to revoke the ban on the Party; and thus, in a few words, unknowingly signed the death sentences in years to come of millions of people in a new World War.

For the Nazis it was a tremendous step forward, but the Catholic alliance upon which it was based alienated Ludendorff, Gregor Strasser and their followers, as well as Count Ernst von Reventlow and Albrecht von Graefe, leaders of the anti-Semitic *Deutsch-Völkische Freiheitspartei* in northern Germany, with whom an electoral alliance had been concluded. It made Party unification harder to achieve.

With unity in mind, Hitler next began to re-establish his own personal dictatorship and to eliminate those who opposed him. Showing a somewhat perverted sense of drama, he staged on 27 February the first mass meeting after his release—the Party's second foundation meeting—

at the Munich Bürgerbräu Cellar, the site of his ill-fated putsch. In a fighting speech which showed he had lost none of his power, he called emotionally for an end to the squabbling which was disrupting the Party, and declared: 'I alone lead the movement, and no one can impose conditions on me so long as I personally bear the responsibility. And I once more bear the whole responsibility for what occurs in the movement.' The re-established Party was now off to the new start which the *Völkischer Beobachter* had announced in a special number the day before.

But the Bavarian and Berlin authorities were watching Hitler. His speech, notably a remark that 'either the enemy marches over our bodies or we march over his,' alarmed them. Early in March they banned Hitler from making public speeches or appearances, first in Bavaria, later in Berlin, and soon in nearly all the German states. In this major setback after a brilliant new start, his main weapon was thus snatched from his hands for more than two years. As a result, he was to occupy himself mainly with completing *Mein Kampf*, strengthening his own position and bolstering Nazi Party organization.

President Ebert died on 25 February 1925. In presidential elections which were to be of great future significance, the Nazis put up General Ludendorff as their candidate against Field-Marshal Hindenburg (Nationalist), Dr Marx (Catholic and Social Democrat) and Ernst Thälmann (Communist). The result was indecisive; worst of all, Ludendorff was revealed as a lost cause, with a mere 285,000 votes out of a total of nearly 27 million.

In the second electoral round, Hitler, in a startling breach of faith, warned his followers to vote instead for

Field-Marshal Hindenburg, and the 78-year-old monarchist and conservative scraped in with 14·6 million votes – rather less than the combined total of his opponents – to preside over the fortunes of the democratic Republic. Eight years later he was to usher the Nazis in to power.

In a private speech to Party leaders in Munich on 27 April 1923, referring to the events which had led to the putsch, Hitler declared: 'What I am fighting is not the State-form in itself, but its shameful content. We wanted to create in Germany the conditions which would alone make it possible that we should be freed from the iron fist of our enemies.

'We wished to bring order into the administration, to drive out the drones, to wage battle against the international Stock Exchange enslavement, against the dominance of the trusts over our whole economic life, against the formation of our trade unions into political bodies, and above all we wanted to see the highest duty which we, as Germans, knew – the duty to bear arms – compulsory military service . . .'

Although he said he wished to free Germany from the domination of international interest-bearing loans and to destroy the power of Germany's great industrial trusts, in practice Hitler allowed the trusts to continue, provided that they collaborated with him. He did, however, refuse foreign interest-bearing loans and tried to obtain necessary imports by barter. He opposed Socialism completely and he was hostile to those Nazis who upheld it.

Meanwhile, voices of dissent were raised against Hitler's drive for supremacy in the Party. Gregor Strasser, a 'Red' Nazi with a tremendous voice, had created for himself a strong following in northern Germany, and he now challenged Hitler's domination, agreeing to collaborate only as a 'fellow worker', and not as a subordinate. In his own newsheets, aided by his brother Otto, he published a programme for a German federation on the Swiss model; the nationalization of heavy industry; the break-up of the great estates, and an end to Prussian militarism.

In every sense opposed to Hitler's policy of collaboration with the industrial magnates, this programme was bound to lead sooner or later to a violent clash. Gregor Strasser engaged as editor of his *National Socialist Newsletter* a young journalist and writer named Josef Goebbels, who revealed his talents as a propagandist as quickly as he was to show his readiness to be a turncoat on a vital issue in the following year.

But in the spring of 1925, Hitler was also beset by the problem of Ernst Röhm, whose *Frontbann*, now 30,000 strong (compared with the 25,000-strong Party), emerged

The first Nazi Party meeting in 1925, in which Hitler reasserted his leadership. Behind Hitler is the famous 'blood banner' of 1923. Sitting on his left are the Party Treasurer, Schwarz, Major Buch of the *Uschla*, and Rosenberg. On his right are Gregor Strasser and his aide, Himmler.

as a serious threat to his struggle for supremacy. Negotiations between the two broke down when Röhm declined Hitler's request that he should bring the *Frontbann* into the Party as the new S.A. and command it under Hitler's undisputed supremacy. On 17 April 1925, Röhm, in a letter to Hitler, resigned his leadership, but having had no answer by 30 April, he wrote another in which, referring to the 'splendid and difficult hours' they had lived through together, he thanked Hitler for his comradeship and asked him 'not to deprive me of your personal friendship'.

Gregor Strasser haranguing a Nazi meeting in northern Germany in 1926. Strasser, who was on the left wing of the Nazi Party, advocated the expropriation of big estates, but Hitler castigated this as 'a Jewish swindle'. Next to Strasser stands the diminutive Josef Goebbels.

Again Hitler made no reply to this staunch friend who had done so much to create the Party, showing once more his indifference to human relationships. Röhm inserted a public announcement about his resignation in the Party newspaper. He lived from hand to mouth from then on, until he secured an appointment as a military adviser in Bolivia.

The conflict with Gregor Strasser also worsened. Strasser's northern German Gauleiters, or district leaders, met in November 1925 and voted for the expropriation of the German princes' estates – a big issue in Germany then – against Hitler, who had condemned the idea as a 'Jewish swindle'. When Gottfried Feder, Hitler's agent at the meeting, protested vehemently on his behalf, Josef Goebbels at once jumped up and demanded that 'the petit bourgeois Adolf Hitler be expelled from the National Socialist Party'.

A flagrant effort at self-promotion by Goebbels, it received little support, but it gave Hitler the chance to organize the defeat of Strasser's breakaway movement. He announced a Gauleiters' conference in the town of Bamberg, Bavaria, where he could speak at a closed meeting and where his supporters would outnumber those of Strasser, who came accompanied only by Goebbels and a few others. In his five-hour speech Hitler condemned Strasser's Socialist policies and called his support for expropriation of the estates 'Marxist'. The intensely ambitious Goebbels quickly saw where his future lay and deserted Strasser in a reply calling for full support for Hitler. He had cut the ground from under Strasser's feet.

It marked a decline in the Strasser opposition and the start of Goebbels' meteoric career, for by the end of 1926 Hitler had appointed him Gauleiter in the Communist stronghold of Berlin.

At the same time, Hitler set up a Party arbitration tribunal under his control named the *Uschla*, to hear and pronounce on any future organizational disputes. It was another step forward in his move towards complete domination of the Party.

Meanwhile, with an eye to his safety and freedom of movement, he had put in hand the formation of a special force to counterbalance the power of the S.A. At first he gave a tough Nazi named Julius Schreck the task of forming the *Schutz Staffeln*, or Safety Squads, soon to be known as the S.S. Ten men and an officer were formed into squads, and one squad each was attached, in theory, to all Party locals throughout Germany. Members of this élite at first wore black ties with their brown shirts, and the skull and crossbones on their black caps to symbolize their readiness to kill and to die for the movement. By early 1926 it was well established, with a carefully chosen membership of several hundred.

The S.A. had now to be reorganized. Hitler appointed Captain Franz Pfeffer von Salomon Commander of the S.A., with effect from 1 November 1926, agreeing to allow him wide powers in his task. It was an error, for soon Pfeffer was following the trail blazed by Röhm, trying to make the S.A. a military force in its own right over which Hitler had little control. Pfeffer also won control of the S.S. before the end of 1926, and promptly limited its strength to 10 per cent of the S.A. This was the start of a bitter rivalry between the two Nazi forces which was not to end until the 1934 bloodbath, when Himmler made the S.S. an all-powerful weapon of terror.

Hitler still hoped to gain power in Germany by means which were at least ostensibly legal, and during the late 1920s the Nazis strengthened and extended their ramifications throughout the country in the hope of attracting enough followers to win power through the ballot box.

A Reich directorate was formed in 1926, a key department officered by Rudolf Hess (Secretary), Franz Xavier Schwartz (Treasurer) and Philipp Bouhler (Secretary-General). Its administrative departments included Agriculture, Economics, Industrial Relations, Foreign Policy, Justice, Interior, Labour, Race and Culture, Science, Press, and lastly, but of importance because Hitler presided over it, Propaganda. Like the shadow cabinet of a parliamentary opposition, the Nazis were thus organized and ready to take power at short notice.

By 1927 the results of this organization were seen in the

A formal portrait of Hitler in S.A. uniform in 1926.

spread of the Party's tentacles in a small way into many important areas of national life. These included the Hitler Youth movement, the National Socialist Student League and the School Pupils' League, as well as professional bodies like the Nazi Teachers' Association, the German Nazi Lawyers' Union, the Nazi Physicians' Union, and the National Socialist Women's League. The numbers of the Gauleiters appointed by Hitler were extended to 34, each of them leader in a region approximating to a Reichstag electoral district.

Party membership was increasing steadily, but only at the rate of between 20,000 and 25,000 a year, so that by 1928 it had grown from about 27,000 in 1925 to slightly over 100,000. Thus the Nazis were at this time still a minority movement, and compared with the Social Democratic Party were insignificant.

In the May 1928 elections, the Nazis, with 810,000 votes, won only 12 seats, including those of Frick, Goebbels, Strasser, General von Epp and Goering, who, recently back from exile in Sweden, had returned happily to the Nazi fold. The Social Democrats polled over nine million votes, and the anti-Republican Nationalists, though dropping two million, still polled over four million votes.

It was a startling defeat—and a measure of Germany's political climate, in which approval of the successes of the Weimar Republic in foreign politics and in restoring prosperity at home was a prominent feature.

In the light of this, Hitler thought another putsch the quickest way to power, but only if he could attract the sure support of the Reichswehr. At a mass meeting on 15 March 1929 he made a plea to the Reichswehr to forget its loyalty oath and to be ready to aid the Nazis in overthrowing the Republic—an invitation to sedition which he persistently followed up in Nazi newspapers.

Reichswehr Minister General Gröner realized that Nazism was fast becoming a real danger to the security of the State. He issued a stern reminder to officers and men about their duty, and the disaster which collaboration with the Nazis would surely cause. Nazi sedition had already infected the Reichswehr; and the trial of three young officers in 1930 for spreading Party propaganda revealed how divided the fighting men's loyalties were between the State and revolutionary feelings.

But Gröner's answer had been a sufficient warning to Hitler. He turned to legality again and worked to

strengthen the Party. Two ambitious young Nazis received vital appointments on 1 January 1929. Both former aides to Gregor Strasser, their industry and ability had already caught Hitler's eye. In Heinrich Himmler, aged 29, overconscientious, asexual and malleable, a fanatical Nazi, a willing tool utterly devoted to the Führer, Hitler saw the man he needed to strengthen the S.S. Deputy Propaganda Chief in 1925, Himmler became Deputy *Reichsführer-S.S.* in 1927 and *Reichsführer-S.S.* in January 1929. He began energetically to build up this formidable instrument of Hitler's will.

The other candidate for power, Josef Goebbels, set his talents as Reich propaganda chief to the creation among other objectives of the pseudo-religious cult of Hitler worship. Thus both Himmler and Goebbels strove in different fields to make Hitler all-powerful.

Meanwhile, Hitler believed that Germany's uncertain prosperity could easily ebb away, and that his chance of power would come when unemployment, only about 650,000 in 1927, rose again and brought a big new influx of the discontented into the Nazi fold. The Party Treasury meantime was bare, but in August 1929, with Foreign Minister Gustav Stresemann's acceptance of the Young Plan for reparations payments (scaled down, but due to last no less than 59 years), came the chance of a big cash inflow, a turning of the financial tide.

The Nazi Party had joined with the Nationalist Party in a furious campaign for a plebiscite on a Bill to stop all future reparations payments. Provided he was given a free hand and substantial funds, Hitler agreed with the Nationalists' leader, the Press and film magnate Alfred Hugenberg, that they should join forces to try to break the Government by declaring in the proposed Bill that the Government would be guilty of treason if it agreed to new reparations payments.

Hugenberg, aged 63, the arch-priest of reaction, called the 'silver fox' because of his cunning and unscrupulousness no less than because of his bristly white hair and moustache, published Hitler's furious attacks on the Government in his newspapers throughout Germany, making his name widely known. But inevitably, the campaign failed. Stresemann died in October 1929, the Reichstag passed the Young Plan and President Hindenburg signed it on 13 March 1930. It provided for the payment of 39,000 million marks, by present value.

Hitler then temporarily broke with the Nationalists and Hugenberg to appease Strasser and his Socialist adherents, who had begun to denounce this close relationship with Germany's old ruling class. But money from Fritz Thyssen, and from Emil Kirdorf, who controlled the Ruhr political

funds and was guest of honour at a march-past of 55,000 Nazis at the August 1929 Nuremberg Party Day, continued for the time being to flow in. Hitler and the Nazis had for a little while won the confidence of the Ruhr magnates.

It was an historic development. Hitler celebrated by re-equipping and enlarging the S.A. and by buying a decaying mansion on Munich's fashionable Briennerstrasse, which he had redesigned as Party Headquarters, with the lugubrious name of the Brown House. Its interior was garishly theatrical – the conference room lined with blood-red leather, the black and scarlet entrance hall showered with swastikas.

Meanwhile, the world economic depression was swiftly making itself felt in Germany. Dependent on foreign, especially U.S., credits and loans, she was hit by a slump when these dried up. Unemployment soared, from 1,320,000 in September 1929 to 3,000,000 in 1930, and to a catastrophic 5,100,000 in 1932. As their painfully rebuilt world began crumbling again, a mood of anger, despair, hate and cynicism gripped the German people.

A sequence of political events followed which paved the way for the death of German democracy. On 27 March 1930 the Müller coalition Government resigned. Heinrich Brüning, schoolmasterly leader of the Catholic Centre party, succeeded him with a programme to cure economic troubles based on deflation and unemployment, but the Nazis and Communists combined in the Reichstag to vote against it.

On 16 July 1930 Brüning therefore took the grave step of persuading President Hindenburg to use his emergency powers under article 48 of the Constitution to give effect to his policy. When in protest his coalition partners refused to vote for him in the Reichstag, he dissolved it and called new elections for 14 September.

A wave of street fighting followed. Among those killed was Horst Wessel, a young Berlin S.A. leader and alleged pimp, who had written a popular Nazi marching song; but he died for non-political reasons – a dispute over a whore. Joyfully, Dr Goebbels turned him into a martyr.

During this wave of violence and murder, 30 million Germans went to the polls, and the results startled the world. The Nazis had become the second biggest party in the Reichstag, with 107 seats, won by 6,409,000 votes. From being a political nuisance, Hitler had overnight soared to commanding status. The Social Democrats remained the biggest party, but the Communists too had grown and were the third biggest.

Hitler's determination to destroy parliamentary democracy had not changed. 'We are a parliamentary party by compulsion and that compulsion is the Constitution,' he declared a few days afterwards. 'I wish to raise once more

Left: Hitler drinks water, while journalists of the Nazi newspaper *Völkischer Beobachter* drink beer, during a Party outing.

Overleaf: Hitler, standing in his 100 m.p.h. Mercedes Benz tourer, and S.A. leader Pfeffer von Salomon, standing on the running board, await the Stormtroopers' march-past at Nuremberg in 1927 as well-wishers' flowers shower down around them. Streicher, in striped tie and gaiters, scowls grimly.

the value of our people . . . We aim to give to this fundamental value, the value of our blood, a logical form, a form
dictated by the highest reason—that means the abolition of
parliamentary democracy.' The 'highest reason' was Hitler's will, which was to be transmitted throughout the
nation by the Nazi system—the Party propagandists, the
S.A. and the S.S.

In 1930, rumblings of discontent and murmurings of
revolt shook the S.A., tired as it was of Hitler's policy of
legality and aching for a bloody revolution. Hitler saw that
decisive action was needed. He sacked Pfeffer, appointed
himself S.A. Supreme Commander and ordered every S.A.
man to swear an oath of unconditional loyalty to him personally. He then recalled Ernst Röhm from Bolivia to take
over as Chief of Staff. With the aid of the S.S., he was then
easily able to crush an abortive S.A. revolt in April 1931.

Under Himmler's leadership the S.S. had grown to some
3,000 men, all of them carefully selected to fit his élitist
philosophy. Hitler ended the arrangement whereby the
S.S. was under overall S.A. control and made it independent, giving it also a distinctive new black uniform and
military organization in companies, battalions, brigades
and divisions, ready for the day he foresaw when it would
be numerous and powerful. Himmler, aided by a talented
newcomer named Reinhardt Heydrich, set up an S.S.
Security Service, the S.D., which grew into the Nazi
secret service, whose role included murder. The S.S. was
on the way to becoming Hitler's weapon for the total
domination of the Party.

In the political field, meanwhile, Chancellor Brüning, at
the start of nearly two years of authoritarian rule without
the Reichstag, was putting his policies into action by presidential decree, despite strong opposition from both Nazis
and Communists. In July 1931 the worsening economic
crisis caused the closure of two big banks; unemployment
came dangerously near the four million level.

As a Stormtrooper formation marches through Berlin in
September 1928, police reinforcements stand by to
prevent street fighting with Communists.

The imminent expiry of President Hindenburg's term of
office was hardly welcome in this grave situation, and
Brüning tried to negotiate an extension of it by requesting
the Nazis to join his coalition to make up the two-thirds
Reichstag majority needful for extending it. But Hitler,
who became a German citizen at this time, and who had
been persuaded by Goebbels and Goering to stand as a
candidate himself, opposed it. The future of Hindenburg,
the one man above all who commanded the Army's loyalty,
was now at stake.

It was a chance for Hitler to become master of Germany
at one blow. But on 13 March 1932 the 84-year-old Field-
Marshal, in a four-cornered fight, polled 18·66 million
votes to Hitler's 11·32 million. In the second election, held
because Hindenburg had failed by a small fraction to win
an absolute majority over all his rivals, Hindenburg's vote
rose to over 19 million and Hitler's to 13·4 million. Hitler
had staged a tremendous fight and had flown hither and
thither across Germany in a small aeroplane to address
tumultuous gatherings of his followers. But Hindenburg
won because a majority of Germans believed he was the
one man able to defend the Republic. They were soon to
be deceived.

Already, in November 1931, Germany had been startled
by the public disclosure of the Boxheim documents, Nazi
plans found during a police search in the manor of Boxheim, in Hesse, for the consolidation of power after a coup.
They included the shooting of political opponents, death
penalties for a wide range of normal political activities and
the suppression of all other parties. It was a symptom of
the sickness of German democracy that little or no effective action was taken against the originators of these
alarming plans for murder and treason.

Heinrich Himmler, aged 30 in this picture, worked
untiringly to make the S.S. the foundation of the Nazi
New Order. He was appointed *Reichsführer S.S.* in 1929,
and by 1931, after an arduous recruiting campaign, had
built up the S.S. into a force containing several
thousand carefully selected men.

In April 1932 Social Democrat Karl Severing, Prussian Minister of the Interior, revealed the discovery of another batch of compromising Nazi documents, including more plans for a blockade of Berlin by the S.A. during a projected Nazi coup. Brüning could no longer evade drastic action. On 14 April 1932 his Reichswehr Minister, General Gröner, banned the S.S., the S.A. and the Hitler Youth. The brown shirts and black uniforms at last vanished from the streets. 'It is exclusively a matter for the State to maintain an organized force,' Gröner belatedly declared. 'As

ward Brüning's successor. He was an obscure deputy of the Prussian parliament named Franz von Papen, a Catholic, rich, aristocratic and part owner of a newspaper, whose narrow, lined, equine face aptly showed his political prejudice. According to von Schleicher's plan, von Papen's Government would try to institutionalize the system of rule by presidential decree, thus stifling democratic government in Germany and establishing a dictatorship.

But first the support of the Bohemian corporal, as Hindenburg liked to call Hitler, had to be obtained, or

Left: The Nationalist leader, Alfred Hugenberg. In 1929 he financed the Nazis in return for Hitler's opposition to the Government's acceptance of the Young Plan for continued war reparations.

Centre: As a Communist demonstration marches past in Munich in 1929, an intense Hitler gives the Nazi salute, Goering (in car) shakes his fist menacingly, and Fritz

Saukel looks ready for trouble. Stormtroopers stand behind the car, prepared for action.

Right: Fritz Thyssen, the millionaire Ruhr industrialist and supporter of Hitler. Beguiled by the Nazi's anti-Bolshevism, he produced large sums of money to help them in their struggle for power.

soon as such a force is organized by private persons and the State permits it, law and order are endangered . . .'

The ban did little to enhance the Government's falling popularity among right-wing groups, and Brüning's scheme to split the big estates of the landowning Junkers into peasant farms turned the landowners against him. Hindenburg, who was one of them, decided to get rid of this tiresome politician, and with him General Gröner, aged 62, who had caused a scandal and offended him by marrying a young woman in her early twenties and only five months later proudly wheeling their newborn son out in his pram.

General Kurt von Schleicher now stepped into the limelight. A born intriguer and womanizer who as chief of the Reichswehr Ministry secretariat dealt on its behalf with the politicians, von Schleicher, in April 1932, told Gröner that his ban on the S.A. had lost him the confidence of the Reichswehr. Dutifully, on 13 May, Gröner resigned; and on 30 May 1932 Brüning, after a stormy interview, heard Hindenburg effectively put an end to his Government with the refusal to grant emergency decrees. He too resigned.

Von Schleicher, in readiness, had already brought for-

von Papen's rule inevitably would be liable to be stormy and short, for the Nazi Party was now over 800,000 strong. Röhm negotiated on Hitler's behalf with his former army comrade, von Schleicher. After much argument a deal was done. In exchange for Nazi support of von Papen, the ban on the S.A., S.S. and Hitler Youth would be lifted, the Nazis would have complete freedom in the streets and, preparatory to new elections, from which the Nazis expected a big advance, the Reichstag would be dissolved.

The Centre Party, however, remained loyal to Brüning and disowned von Papen who, by 2 June 1932, formed a so-called non-party Government, the 'Cabinet of barons'. It was unpopular throughout Germany, but von Schleicher, as Reichswehr Minister, brought to it the Army's valuable support.

Growls of anger arose among the Socialist Nazis led by Gregor Strasser at this deal with a man who stood for everything which they hated in the old order. While Hitler looked for friends among magnates, Strasser was violently attacking the shortcomings of capitalism, calling it 'a degenerate economic system'. This stark contrast in outlook was bound sooner or later to end in conflict.

Democracy now vanished for good in Prussia, and not with a bang, but a whimper. At von Papen's suggestion Hindenburg had appointed him Reich Commissioner for Prussia in place of the Social Democratic Government led by Karl Severing. On 10 July 1932 a state of emergency was declared there, backed up by Reichswehr armoured fighting vehicles and troops. Prussia's well-armed police stood by in readiness, but Severing's Cabinet left office with only a mild protest and not the slightest resistance.

The Nazis now brought to the all-Germany election campaign the maximum of energy, in a stream of torch-light parades, inflammatory speeches and acts of terrorism in more than a hundred towns. After the all too brief six weeks' ban, the Stormtroopers' street warfare was once more unleashed. From 1 June to mid-July 1932, some 70 people were killed and nearly 500 badly wounded. In Altona near Hamburg on 17 July another 17 people were killed when a mob of S.A. descended on a Communist stronghold.

The election's last great rally was staged at the end of July in Berlin's vast Grünewald Stadium. 'Picked men from the *Schutz Staffeln* were drawn up in close ranks below the stand,' noted Kurt Ludecke, who was there.

Top: Jackbooted Stormtroopers hold steel-tipped clubs aloft in salute as they march past Hitler, Goebbels and Goering at Nuremberg in 1929.

Right: Goebbels, flanked by a grim-faced unit of Stormtroopers, delivers a speech in Freienwalde in September 1929.

Top: Police search Stormtroopers for hidden weapons. The police could do little to prevent the savage clashes between Communists and Nazis in the early 30s.

Bottom: Hitler addresses a crowd at the grave of Horst Wessel, a young Stormtrooper and composer of a Nazi marching song, who was killed in the election fighting in 1930.

Top: Hitler emerges from an election meeting in Munich in September 1930 too exhausted to respond to Nazi salutes. The elections followed the defeat of Brüning's Government in the Reichstag and were accompanied by savage street fighting between Nazis and Communists.

Bottom: Ernst Röhm inspects members of the S.A. in 1930 after his return from Bolivia, where he had been serving with the Bolivian Army. Hitler had persuaded him to return as S.A. Chief of Staff.

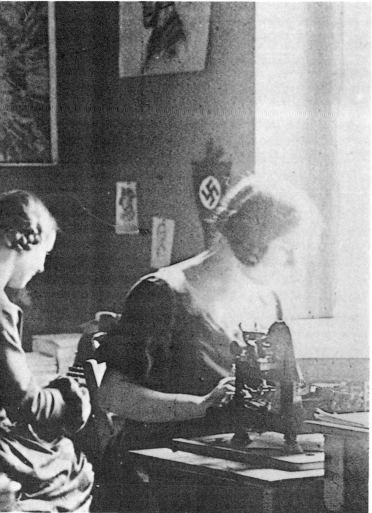

'Twelve huge S.A. bands played military marches with beautiful precision and terrifying power. Behind the bands, on the field itself, solid squares of uniformed men from the Nazi labour unions were ranged in strict military order, thousands strong . . . Suddenly a wave surged over the crowd . . . Hitler is coming! Hitler is here! A blare of trumpets rent the air, and a hundred thousand people leaped to their feet in tense expectancy . . . There was a low rumble of excitement and then, releasing its pent up emotion, the crowd burst into a tremendous ovation, the "Heils" swelling until they were like the roar of a mighty cataract.

'Hitler had stepped through a passage-way on to the tribune, bathed in light, hatless, brown-shirted, briskly saluting. When the tumult subsided . . . he threw defiance and appeal with his whipping, cracking speech . . .'

The elections next day were a Nazi landslide. With 13·7 million votes out of a total of 36·8 million, the Party captured 230 seats compared with the Social Democrats' 133 seats, the Communists' 89, and 147 split among the seven other parties. Von Papen should now, according to precedent, have resigned, and President Hindenburg should have offered Hitler the Chancellorship, but this did not happen. Hindenburg was reported as saying, 'Never will I make the Bohemian corporal Chancellor!' Von Papen continued to rule by emergency decree.

Hitler was furious. Suspense gripped the whole country. The S.A., angry at this slight on their leader and contemptuous of his unrewarding policy of 'legality', swarmed into the streets again and a wave of shooting, bombing and stabbing swept through cities and towns. The S.A. then ringed Berlin, while Hitler and Röhm hinted that they were almost out of control. Von Papen replied by promulgating on 9 August a law carrying the death penalty for terrorism.

Hitler then met von Schleicher and told him that he would accept nothing less than total and absolute control of the State. A week later there were still no positive developments. Ironically, it was President Hindenburg who was now playing an illegal game, while Hitler, despite all the aces he held – the favour of the Reichswehr, the 650,000-strong S.A., Nazi provincial governments in five states – clung desperately to legality.

Then, on 13 August 1932, together with Röhm and Frick, he answered Hindenburg's summons to the palace. It was the answer to Hitler's request for an interview two days earlier. A frosty reception awaited them. Hindenburg received them standing, leaning heavily on his stick. Bluntly, he demanded that Hitler should agree to serve in von Papen's Government as Vice-Chancellor. No less

Above, left: Hitler confers with Stormtrooper leaders after the Nazis had gained power in the province of Thuringia in 1931, their first victory. Röhm's scarred face is visible to the right of Hitler.

Above, right: A grim-faced Hitler inspects units of Stormtroopers and S.S. men during the run-up to the 1931 elections.

Left: Josef Goebbels confers with a senior S.A. officer, *Gruppenführer* Stennes. By 1930 Goebbels had risen to be both Party Propaganda Director and Gauleiter of Berlin.

Above, left: In April 1932 the Reichswehr Minister, General Gröner, banned the S.A. and S.S. For a brief period they were forced to abandon their uniforms. Here Hitler reviews a mass meeting in the Sportpalast of the Berlin Nazi Party, who are assembled in civilian dress.

Above: Heinrich Brüning, the donnish leader of the Catholic Centre Party, addresses the Reichstag in 1932. His Coalition Government was brought down in May 1932 by the intriguing of General von Schleicher.

Left: General von Schleicher, the successor to General Gröner, confers with Röhm's aide, Count Spreti. Schleicher struck a bargain with Röhm, who acted for Hitler, to lift the ban on the S.A. and S.S. in return for Nazi support for the new von Papen Government.

bluntly, Hitler refused: he wanted absolute power or nothing. Hindenburg declared that he could not reconcile his duty to the Fatherland with giving power to a party so dependent on violence. The interview was at an end. Hitler had been snubbed.

For the moment, the Nazis, manœuvred into a political blind alley, had lost. Seizure of power by armed force was ruled out, while power was denied them though they had fought and won 'legally'. What was left? Only Hitler's insensate will to fight on until he had outflanked von Papen, von Schleicher and Hindenburg, and had somehow become Chancellor by legal means.

But the humiliation Hindenburg had inflicted upon him dented his popularity, and he began to be considered a falling star. Then in August came the affair of the Potempa murderers. Five S.A. men had been condemned to death on 22 August 1932 for kicking a miner, a Communist, to death—a brutal killing which had been widely publicized. Hitler was now faced with the choice of letting the murderers die and alienating the whole S.A. or intervening on their behalf and alienating public opinion.

He chose the latter course and secured the reduction of their sentences to life imprisonment, but it was a victory over von Papen of doubtful value, for public opinion was clearly disgusted by it, especially by the further weakening of the law in its role of citizen's guardian.

Instead of biding his time now, and letting von Papen's 'Cabinet of barons' dig its own grave, Hitler ordered Goering, who on 30 August had been elected Reichstag president, to bring about von Papen's defeat there at once and at all costs—believing that Hindenburg could then do

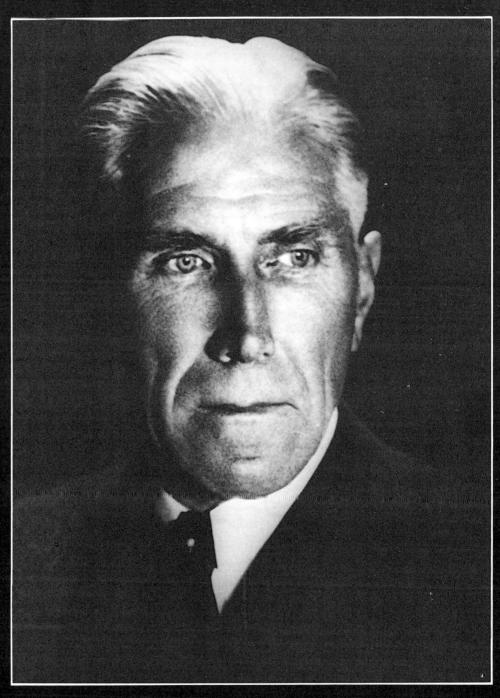

Franz von Papen, Brüning's successor as Chancellor, was a pawn in the intrigues of Von Schleicher. Of his appointment as Chancellor, von Papen later remarked, 'It more or less represented the vote of the Army.'

Left: A Nazi election poster of 1932: it plays on the public dread of unemployment and hunger—'Our Last Hope: HITLER.'

Centre: This Communist election poster of 1932

symbolizes the aggressive Communist response to the threat of Nazism.

Right: This Nazi election poster urges voters to 'smash the world's enemy'—international high finance.

no other than turn to him. It was a serious mistake. On 12 September 1932, the Reichstag assembly day, Goering succeeded in massing an overwhelming vote of 513 to 32 on a Communist vote of no confidence in the Government. But now, instead of resigning, von Papen dissolved the Reichstag, fixed new elections for 6 November and meantime ruled by presidential decree. He was certain that for the Nazis the electoral tide was ebbing. On a foggy, wintry day the weary electorate trudged to the polling booths for the fifth time in recent months, feeling, as the results showed, that perhaps after all the Nazis could do little for them. The Party lost 34 seats and two million votes, the Communists gained 12 seats, reaching 100, and the Nationalists gained ten.

The adroit von Papen moved to exploit this Nazi setback by offering Hitler the bait of the Vice-Chancellorship again, hoping to tie his hands. Hitler firmly refused it, with the public declaration that von Papen's reactionary policy of government by decree had increased the Communist vote and opened the door to Bolshevism. Von Schleicher knew this to be true and he now believed that the von Papen experiment had failed. He therefore induced von Papen to resign to try to end the deadlock. Hindenburg then gave Hitler the chance of forming a stable coalition government, knowing full well that such an attempt would be stillborn, with its sure rejection by the Nationalists and the Centre Party. And so it was.

Von Papen now stood ready for the role of dictator, with the backing of the Reichswehr's bayonets, but von Schleicher firmly told his protégé that, faced by the possibility of a simultaneous rising of both Nazis and Communists, the Reichswehr had lost confidence in him. It was no less a humiliation than that which von Papen had handed Hitler by refusing to resign in his favour after the July elections. Von Papen's vanity was deeply wounded;

and from that moment he looked for a chance of revenge on von Schleicher.

Displeased at the exit of the urbane and aristocratic von Papen, of whom he had grown fond, Hindenburg reluctantly accepted von Schleicher's proposal of himself as Chancellor, and the arch-intriguer took office on 3 December 1932. He was fated to be the last democratic Chancellor in Germany's stormy postwar history. And his every act now seemed to hasten the change, as though destiny was in a hurry.

First, in a move to try to topple Hitler for good, and to attract radical elements so as to split the Nazis, von Schleicher offered the post of Vice-Chancellor to Gregor Strasser, the second man in the Party hierarchy. As its organizer since 1925, Strasser possessed a strong following of what were called the Nazi idealists. He readily agreed, but was obliged to put the matter to Hitler, who, seeing in him a rival for supreme power, refused adamantly.

Strasser thereupon wrote Hitler a letter violently attacking his direction of the Nazi Party, predicting chaos and ruin for Germany if it continued, and finally resigning his various offices. Without a word to anyone, and with victory almost in his grasp, he then went off on holiday with his family to Italy.

The event provoked a serious split among the leading members of the Nazi hierarchy. Most of the parliamentary group, including Wilhelm Frick, supported Strasser, and urged Hitler to compromise in the present grave situation.

Opposite, top: Ernst Thälmann (left), the leader of the Communist Red Front, at the head of a march in 1932. He was arrested and imprisoned in 1933 and died in a concentration camp in 1944.

Opposite, bottom: Police break up street fighting between Communists and Nazi students near Berlin University in March 1932.

Goering and Himmler hurry to the Reichstag on 12 December 1932, the day the Nazis voted with the Communists to defeat von Papen's 'government of barons'.

Hitler greets the ageing President von Hindenburg at a memorial service following Hitler's appointment as Chancellor on 30 January 1933.

But during the hiatus caused by Strasser's absence, Hitler seized his chance, attacked him for his threat to Party unity, broke up his caucus and rallied the Party round him with a New Year's Day declaration that he would never sell its independence by taking part in a Government without real power.

He won the day, but now a financial crisis threatened to bankrupt the Nazis and bring them down, for their total debts were reported to be no less than 12 million marks. The Stormtroopers were shaking collecting boxes under the noses of passers-by in the streets to try to raise enough money to keep their canteens in fuel and food. The costs of so many elections and the drying up of donations from the doubting magnates had emptied Franz Xavier Schwartz's Party treasury.

On all sides worried looks were exchanged. Goebbels even mentioned in public his fears of the movement's collapse. 'Acute depression prevails in the organisation,' he wrote in his diary in December. 'Financial worries render all systematic work impossible. Everybody is in a very despondent mood.'

In a desperate attempt to stave off financial collapse and attract help, Hitler and his top men put the word around that if the Nazis failed, Germany would be faced with ten million more Communists overnight. This coincided with a determined move by the still angry von Papen to reach a compromise with Hitler, then to form a coalition government supported by the industrialist magnates and at the same time revenge himself on von Schleicher by bringing about his fall. On 4 January 1933 Hitler and von Papen met secretly at the house of a pro-Nazi banker, Baron Kurt von Schröder, near Cologne. The Nazis' chance was coming.

More reasonable, in view of his urgent financial worries, than he had been, Hitler agreed in principle with von Papen on the formation of a coalition with the Nationalists to form a government and force von Schleicher out. At the same time, von Schröder made arrangements to settle most of the Party's debts and brought the assurance of renewed backing from sections of heavy industry, who saw in the plan their last chance of a Government able to stop a Communist coup.

Von Schleicher at this time was in trouble with both Hindenburg and the Nationalist Party over the influential Land League's protest about his policy of breaking up and settling the big estates, which it called 'agrarian Bolshevism'. Secretly, Hindenburg had authorized von Papen to prepare an alternative 'national concentration' coalition Government including the Nazis.

A column of Stormtroopers march singing through Berlin on 30 January 1933 to celebrate Hitler's appointment as Chancellor.

Already meetings were taking place between Hitler and Hugenberg, von Papen and Oskar von Hindenburg, the President's son, at Joachim von Ribbentrop's house, to bargain for and allocate power in the coalition. Hugenberg at first would not agree to grant Hitler more than the Vice-Chancellorship, but he later gave in to von Papen's insistence that Hitler be made Chancellor—provided that von Papen was Vice-Chancellor. Agreement was reached.

On 28 January the situation reached a climax. Von Schleicher requested Hindenburg to grant him emergency powers so that he could govern by decree, without the Reichstag. Hindenburg refused. Von Schleicher now had no alternative but to resign, for the Reichstag was against him. Von Papen, having finally settled his Cabinet by naming himself Reich Commissioner for Prussia, which Hitler had wanted, obtained Hindenburg's hesitant agreement to it on the morning of 29 January 1933. Hindenburg's decision seems to have been hastened by rumours, later known to have been manufactured, that von Schleicher intended to call out the Reichswehr and seize power by force.

The next day, 30 January 1933, in the solemn ritual in the Reich Chancellery at noon, tragedy blended uneasily with farce. Adolf Hitler stood in his morning coat before Field-Marshal Paul von Hindenburg, and Franz von Papen confirmed that a Government of 'national concentration' had been formed, in which Hitler would be Chancellor and he himself Vice-Chancellor. Both he and Hindenburg believed, despite the history of the past decade, that von Papen and Hugenberg would be the real rulers and Hitler the front man, caged at last. Their awakening would not be delayed for long.

Hindenburg took in his big gnarled had Hitler's almost feminine one and swore him in as Chancellor. Then Hitler firmly repeated the oath of loyalty to the Weimar Republic, which he had vowed to destroy. He planned to do this at once.

That night, a vast torchlight procession of militarized columns of S.A., S.S. and *Stahlhelm* marched past the cheering crowds, and the Berlin streets echoed to their heavy tread, mingled with the menacing rhythm of massed military bands. Hindenburg looked on with wooden approval from his window on the Wilhelmstrasse, and nearby, in the Kaiserhof, a beaming Adolf Hitler threw up his arm endlessly in the Nazi salute.

Equipped with the twin forces of terror and legality, the Nazis now put into action their plans to overwhelm the nation with a pitiless revolution. Incredibly, Hitler had reached the pinnacle of power in Germany. He was now to use this power to destroy every vestige of political freedom.

83

NAZI ART AND ARCHITECTURE
Mirror of the New Germany

Hitler's will and taste rigidly controlled art and architecture in Nazi Germany. The Führer had convinced himself that had he not become the nation's leader in politics he could have attained great heights as an architect since he was at heart an artist. Therefore no buildings of any importance could be built, and no sculpture or paintings put on public display, unless they conformed to that which Hitler had ordained was German in nature—even though this decree ran counter to the true national genius in impressionistic and expressionistic painting, or the great simplicity of outstanding architects like Gropius. The penalty for disobedience, for not conforming, was a spell in a concentration camp.

The artistic ideas, feelings and prejudices which Hitler imposed on Germany were in essence those of the average man—lacking somewhat in sensibility and knowledge. Hitler ordained that in both form and content paintings were to be strictly representational and were to display an exact fidelity to nature, a photographic likeness to reality. Abstract art like that of Bracque or Picasso, or the brilliant expressionism of Oscar Kokoschka, were castigated as un-German and therefore could have no place in the new Germany. Hitler also censured the internationalization of art, insisting that Nazi art must spring from Germany's 'sacred earth'. According to Albert Speer, Hitler's own favourite paintings were of laughing red-nosed friars, gulping down quarts of ale, executed with loving attention to detail by a minor German painter named Eduard Grützner.

Just as the nineteenth century was the source of his taste in art, so it was in architecture. Hitler particularly cared for the German neo-baroque style. Despite this pre-

Top left: The Chancellery in Berlin

Above centre: The conference hall in the Castle 'Bellevue', a Nazi guest house for visiting diplomats.

Right: Hitler impassively studies a reclining figure representing German womanhood. Hitler denounced the internationalization of art and called for German art based on simple realism.

Top right: The German pavilion at the Paris World's Fair in 1937. Designed by Albert Speer, it was surmounted by the Nazi eagle and a swastika.

dilection, he gave way to the promptings of Albert Speer, and a spare but ponderous neo-classical style, favoured originally by the architect Paul Ludwig Troost, became what could be called the official style of the Third Reich. Hitler also insisted that public buildings had to be monumental in style, so that the spirit of Nazism would shine out from them for the edification of future generations. The vast size of Hitler's public buildings—often bigger than anything ancient or modern anywhere—reflected both his pride in the Party and his urge to dominate the world. Speer relates in his autobiography that he persuaded Hitler to allow him to design buildings also for the look they would have as ruins. And Hitler agreed, thinking of the glories that were Greece.

Top right: The German pavilion at the Paris World's Fair in 1937. Designed by Albert Speer, it was surmounted by the Nazi eagle and a swastika.

Hitler Imposes a Revolution

Hitler's first Cabinet. Hitler talks impatiently to Goering, von Papen (sitting, right) already appears an outsider, and Hugenberg looks apprehensive. Next to Hugenberg is General von Blomberg, then Wilhelm Frick, Schwerin Krosigk, Gercke and Franz Seldte.

True for any other party would have been Franz von Papen's belief that the Nazis were tied hand and foot by filling only three seats out of eleven in the new coalition Government in January 1933—Hitler as Chancellor, Goering as Minister without Portfolio (and Prussian Minister of the Interior) and the quietly formidable Wilhelm Frick as Minister of the Interior. But von Papen was incapable of either political or psychological insight.

Von Papen was Vice-Chancellor and Reich Commissioner for Prussia. Hugenberg, the Nationalist leader, held the portfolios of Trade, and of Food and Agriculture; Franz Seldte, leader of the Nationalist *Stahlhelm* force, held that of Labour, while Hindenburg had chosen Baron von Neurath as Foreign Minister and General Werner von Blomberg for the vital post of Reichswehr Minister. To rightists of his own choice von Papen had allocated the remaining posts.

It seemed enough to keep the Nazis caged. But unfortunately von Papen had failed to discern that both von Blomberg and Dr Franz Gürtner, Minister of Justice, were Nazi sympathizers. Seldte was hardly a reliable ally and Goering, with over half a million S.A. to call upon, was unlikely to let von Papen stand in his way in Prussia.

Von Papen's hopes therefore were doomed from the start, for the Nazis were determined on nothing less than total power. So swiftly did they move to rid themselves of political opposition—by legal means backed always by the threat of terrorism—that in five months Hitler was to become German dictator, while all political parties except the Nazi Party were to vanish from national life.

In the revolution that began, fundamental changes occurred with phenomenal speed. On 31 January 1933 Hitler and von Papen together persuaded President Hindenburg to dissolve the Reichstag at once until after the new elections, scheduled for five weeks later, on 5 March 1933. Hitler expected then to win many more seats than the present Nazi–Nationalist coalition of 247 out of a total of 583, so that he could then put his startling programme through without having to concede anything to other parties.

But in these five weeks before the elections, the Government, ruling by decree, was to obtain the bewildered Hindenburg's signature to a stream of laws which overturned the entire democratic system and began to make an authoritarian state of Germany. Hitler heralded it on 1 February 1933 at a gathering of naval and military chiefs. He declared that the nation's political life would be changed by force, that democracy, pacifism and Marxism would be suppressed and replaced by authoritarian rule. Conscription would be introduced, youth would again be taught love for bearing arms, and weapons production would be increased with a view to solving Germany's economic problems by conquest and settlement in eastern Europe and Russia. It was the fullest and frankest statement of his political aims to a non-party audience so far. The generals were pleased. Hitler had won the Reichswehr's political neutrality.

The predicted onslaught on democracy began at once.

Goering issued an order prohibiting all Communist demonstrations in Prussia; and on 4 February 1933 Hindenburg signed the Government's so-called Decree for the Protection of the German People. It gave the police Draconian powers to suppress any publication and any public meeting they considered a danger to public security, as well as to imprison anyone who organized or even attended any such meeting, or who failed to report the existence of any forbidden publication of which they were aware. Strikes in important industries were also prohibited. With one stroke, and within a week of Hitler's becoming Chancellor, dangerous inroads upon the citizen's freedom and security had been made.

But this was only the beginning. On 14 February 1933, Goering sternly warned the Prussian police, who had opposed terrorism in the streets, against 'hostility' towards the S.A., S.S. or *Stahlhelm*. He went on to say that if the police should use firearms while keeping public order they would be fully protected by him; those who failed to take such action would be punished. Put briefly, it meant that the police had either to shoot political demonstrators, or be punished for not shooting.

Continuing his plan to gain control of the police, Goering next day engineered the removal of the police chiefs of Berlin and twelve other Prussian cities, putting in their places S.A. or S.S. men, or Nazi sympathizers, thus starting the transformation of higher police echelons into a branch of the Nazi Party. These moves went on against a background of revolver shots and the smack of truncheons, as Stormtroopers attacked election meetings of rival parties, including one of the Catholic Centre Party addressed by ex-Chancellor Heinrich Brüning. When Catholic newspapers in Prussia published a combined protest by Church organizations, Goering added them to the long list of newspapers already suppressed either temporarily or permanently.

On 22 February 1933 Nazism achieved complete domination over Germany's police forces. Goering mobilized 50,000 S.S., S.A. and *Stahlhelm* in Prussia alone as an auxiliary force not subject to the same restraining traditions and rules as the regular police. The auxiliaries were simply given revolvers, batons and a white armband marked 'special' to wear over their brownshirts or black tunics; they were paid only three marks a day and sent into the streets to aid other S.A. and S.S. thugs in their role of crushing political liberty. It gave them licence for any and every kind of violence, about which the citizen complained to the regular police at his peril. Goering had thus degraded the role of the police in society and robbed the ordinary citizen of police protection. It was a move which struck fear into the hearts of all non-Nazi Germans, who were in the majority, and, since any opposition now involved great physical danger, made the run-up to the elections much more of a one-way campaign.

Hitler, Goering and Röhm head the column marching behind President Hindenburg after the ceremony in the Garrison Church, Potsdam, on 21 March 1933 to celebrate the opening of the Nazi régime's first Reichstag, and to mark the 'new unity' of Germany.

But more funds were still needed to achieve the kind of victory upon which Hitler was resolved. On 20 February 1933, Goering arranged a meeting of hand-picked industrial magnates and big bankers, including Baron von Schröder, who had settled Nazi debts in December and had played a vital role in Hitler's becoming Chancellor. Hitler gave them the policy speech to which he had already treated the Army and Navy chiefs, and Hjalmar Schacht, acting as treasurer, solicited contributions to the election fund that would enable this policy to become reality. There was no lack of enthusiasm among them for the Nazis now. There and then the magnates and bankers produced promissory notes and cheques totalling about three million marks.

On the evening of 27 February, barely a week before the elections, came an incident so favourable for the Nazis, at a time when criticism of them was mounting, that they were mistakenly believed to have engineered it themselves. At 9.15 p.m. clouds of smoke were seen billowing from the Reichstag building and soon the great dome itself was in flames. In an untouched part of the building police arrested a Dutch stonemason named van der Lubbe, aged 24, who at once admitted to having caused the blaze, and to being a Communist. Hitler and Goering rushed to the scene, inwardly rejoicing as flame and sparks rose up into the night air. They now had a valuable and much-needed pretext for launching the ruthless action they had already planned against their formidable and well-organized opponents the Communists.

Next morning the *Völkischer Beobachter* warned Germany that the fire was the signal for a wave of Communist sabotage and terrorism, leading up to a *coup d'état* and a subsequent reign of terror—all of which, however, existed only in Hitler's fertile mind. Goering placed the entire Prussian police force in a state of emergency, as if acting to defend the Reich from these dangerous internal enemies. He also suppressed for a month all Communist, and for two weeks all Socialist media in Prussia—none of them, in fact, was ever allowed to publish again. In the afternoon Hitler presented to Hindenburg for signature, and later promulgated, an emergency decree, 'in Defence of the People and the State'. It drove a coach and horses through the Weimar Constitution, suspending entirely the seven articles—already limited by the 4 February decree—which guaranteed the citizen's security in his own home and his liberty. The German people was thus deprived of freedom of speech, of the Press, of association and assembly; of privacy of the post, telephone, telegraph, of guarantees against house searches without warrant, and of confiscation of property. The decree also authorized the Government to assume full powers in any of the German States, and enforced the death penalty instead of life imprisonment for high treason, causing an explosion, arson, sabotage and poisoning, as well as for conspiracy to assassinate Government members, for seizing hostages, and for grave breaches of the peace under arms, or with someone armed. A big step towards the absolute tyranny of Nazism had been taken.

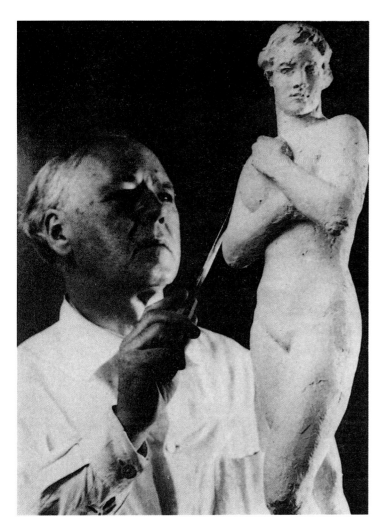

Opposite, left: Hitler (right) in formal civilian dress, with General von Blomberg, an aide and Vice-Chancellor von Papen, answers a few final questions after telling a meeting of generals and admirals on 1 February 1933 that the armed forces were to be quickly expanded.

Opposite, right: The Reichstag building in Berlin bursts into flames at 9.15 p.m. on 27 February 1933. While the fire was still spreading, the police arrested a young Dutch Communist named van der Lubbe. The arrest of Communist leaders, including the Bulgarian Dimitroff, followed at once. But the subsequent trial misfired; the Communist leaders were acquitted and released, leaving the unhappy van der Lubbe to be hurriedly executed.

Left: Professor Kolbe, an officially 'German' sculptor, models the broad-shouldered, wide-hipped 'German Woman and Mother'.

of the Nationalists they had 340 seats out of a Reichstag total of 647, a majority of only 33, and far from the overwhelming public affirmation for which they had hoped. Hardly 52 per cent of the electorate had voted for them; and without the Nationalists they had no majority at all.

Nevertheless, as a propaganda move, the Nazis spoke of it in public as a great victory, and Goering declared himself grateful that the German people had acclaimed Hitler's Chancellorship by such an overwhelming majority. Privately they had to accept that it was a rebuff, and terrorism was from this time on intensified in accord with Hitler's belief in its coercive power.

Nazi rather than Government control over the whole of Germany was now tightened by the appointment in the next few days of all-powerful Governors, or Commisioners, in the States, directly responsible to the Minister of the Interior, Wilhelm Frick. Von Papen was, of course, already commissioner for Prussia.

Naked force accompanied these ruthless actions. Cities throughout Germany echoed to the heavy tread of long columns of brown-shirted Stormtroopers, who, after forcing their way into the States' Government offices on the new Commissioners' behalf, went on to shatter and loot the Catholic and Social Democratic newspaper offices and printing presses, and the trade union headquarters, as well as to beat up the staff.

Bavaria at first firmly refused to accept this theft of its rights and threatened violence to any Nazi Commissioners who attempted to take over. Plans were afoot there for a restoration of the monarchy, but eventually Dr Heinrich Held was forced to capitulate. He promptly sought refuge in Switzerland, but his son was later flung into a concentration camp for refusing to divulge the whereabouts of his father. For Held the savage irony of this tragedy was that it was he who, in 1925, after Hitler's release from prison, had thoughtlessly revoked the total ban on the Nazis in Bavaria, thus enabling Hitler to reorganize his shattered party. General Franz Ritter von Epp, Röhm's former commanding officer, and a secret supporter of Hitler in Munich in the early 1920s, was appointed Reich Commissioner for Bavaria.

Heinrich Himmler, who at this time was smarting from his Führer's ungrateful disregard of him in failing to reward his labours on behalf of the S.S., was appointed Munich police chief by von Epp. A sharp rise in arrests of Social Democrats and Communists followed as Himmler

Spurning protests, Goering declared on 3 March 1933: 'My business is not to dispense justice but to destroy and exterminate, beyond that nothing.' Like a lightning flash at night, it shed sudden light on the Nazi commitment to evil and Goering's philosophy of destruction.

It was in this atmosphere—violence on the streets, suppression of rival political meetings, paralysis of the police, armed Stormtroopers' marches by torchlight through every city and town with huge and threatening swastika banners, and doubts in the public mind that the ballot was any longer secret—that the elections took place on Sunday, 5 March 1933. But despite this background, and with a record of nearly 90 per cent of the electorate voting, the Nazis still failed to get the really resounding victory for which they had fought.

Out of a total of some 39,343,000 votes, the Nazi vote increased by some 5·5 million to 17,277,300, or 43·9 per cent, compared with their 33·1 per cent in November 1933. The Nationalists' vote increased by only 180,000 to 3,136,000; while the Catholic Centre Party managed to push up from 4,230,600 to 4,244,900. The Communists, tied hand and foot, dropped about a million votes, with a total of 4,848,100; the Social Democrats, with 7,181,000, lost 66,400 votes.

The voting thus gave the Social Democrats 120 seats, which was one less than in November; the Communists 81, or 19 less; the Centrists 73, or three more; the five small parties a total loss of several seats; and the Nazis 288 seats, which was a gain of 96. Combined with the 52 seats

strove for recognition with all the methodical persistence of an overconscientious filing clerk.

Anxious always to bring himself to the notice of his adored Führer, Himmler now began to discover imaginary plots on Hitler's life. They coincided with Hitler's growing anxiety, which never left him, about assassins lurking everywhere to slay him. Pondering on the best protection, the name of the reliable Himmler naturally came to mind, and he sent him an order to form immediately a head-quarters guard of specially chosen men who would be sworn to lay down their lives if need be in his defence.

Himmler felt the Führer's choice of him for this vital task was a great honour, and with more than his usual methodical care he studied his S.S. dossiers in search of a man with the right balance of initiative, ruthlessness and reliability.

He recommended, and Hitler accepted, the Bavarian *S.S.-Gruppenführer* Sepp Dietrich–later to rise to eminence as General of a *Panzer* army–who had served Hitler earlier as a bodyguard commander. Dietrich formed a company of 120 carefully chosen S.S. men and Hitler named it the *Leibstandarte-S.S. Adolf Hitler*–the Adolf Hitler Bodyguard.

The event was a breakthrough towards the Nazi hierarchy for Himmler, and early in April he was appointed Commander of Bavaria's Political Police. Between him and Goering, who was in charge of the entire Prussian police, conflict was now certain, for Himmler, intensely ambitious, was already quietly planning a unified nation-wide police force, of which he saw himself as supreme chief.

Meanwhile, in March, the first concentration camps had already been set up, as the Nazi régime quickly began materially to reflect the hate, violence and terrorism in Hitler's mind. The first, at Oranienburg, near Berlin, was under Goering's jurisdiction; the camp at Dachau in Bavaria, north of Munich, in the bare surroundings of the old stone barns of a disused explosives factory, was under Himmler's control.

The first batches of prisoners–some Socialist and Communist Reichstag deputies, three or four thousand Communists arrested after the Reichstag fire, and soon Jews, Social Democrats and Catholics–were thrown pell-mell into what later became infernos of cruelty, in which only the fortunate few survived.

Terrorism and punishment were the foundation of the régime: severe beatings and torture were handed out by guards carefully chosen for their immunity to feelings of pity or humanity, and taught to hate the inmates unmercifully. Semi-starvation, exhausting labour, lack of proper sanitation and medical treatment, the grossest overcrowding–these were normal. The camps mushroomed

Opposite, top: In March 1933 the first prisoners arrived at the Oranienburg concentration camp near Berlin. Habitual criminals preceded political prisoners, and at first the régime in the camp was based upon official German prison rules and was not inhuman.

Opposite, bottom: Hitler Youth standard bearers head a mass parade in Munich in the spring of 1933.

up all over Germany, and later, of course, in the occupied countries as well.

Prisoners began to die in unexplained circumstances. Officials of the Ministry of Justice, among whom a proper regard for Germany's normal prison regulations still survived, protested to Himmler. Usually they were informed that the Führer did not wish the camp régime to be altered. Hermann Rauschning, Nazi leader in Danzig in 1933, was present when moderates in the Party drew Hitler's attention to the cruelties which were under way.

Instead of ordering an immediate end to such barbarism, Hitler flew into a rage with the individuals who had

Close-cropped prisoners parade in Dachau in 1933. Himmler's first concentration camp was then called a 'training camp'. Severity, cruelty and inhumanity ousted the standard German prison régime when Hitler caused brutal and sadistic S.A. guards to be put in charge.

'made a fuss' about it, his face purple and distorted, his mouth foaming. 'Why babble about brutality and be indignant about tortures?' he shouted. 'The masses want that. They need something that will give them a thrill of horror. I forbid you to change anything. By all means punish one or two men, so that these German Nationalist donkeys may sleep easy. But I don't want the concentration camps changed into penitentiary institutions. Terror is the most effective political instrument. I shall not permit myself to be robbed of it simply because a lot of stupid, bourgeois mollycoddles choose to be offended by it ... People will think twice about opposing us when they hear what to expect in the camps. It's your business to see that no evidence about such cases leaks out. I cannot allow such absurd trifles to break in on my work. Anybody who is such a poltroon that he cannot bear the thought of someone nearby having to suffer pain had better join a sewing circle, but not my Party comrades.'

Brutality and torture–to inflict them was a primitive and horrifying drive in Hitler. It was said to have been caused by his wish for revenge for the suffering he had allegedly experienced in his youth–as if society was the guilty source of it. This is hardly convincing; countless men genuinely suffer in their youth. It is unlikely that a man of Hitler's extraordinary, but twisted intelligence would have reacted to the frustrations of his younger days in such a shallow and virulent way as to torture for

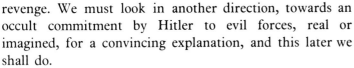

revenge. We must look in another direction, towards an occult commitment by Hitler to evil forces, real or imagined, for a convincing explanation, and this later we shall do.

Nazi leaders and officials, from the top of the hierarchy down to the humble *S.S.-Obersturmführer* (lieutenant), were infected by Hitler's obsessions; though, as will be seen, there were important exceptions. Himmler was one of those of whom Hitler's demon had seemingly taken total possession; Goering, now in the grip of morphine addiction, was another. Both, in 1933, worked furiously to add to their own dominions by creating, in Bavaria and Prussia respectively, ruthless Nazi police states.

In March 1933 Himmler added to his infant police empire Special S.S. Detachments (*S.S.-Sonderkommandos*) which later were to grow into the coldblooded butchers of civilians in occupied Russia, whose atrocities even the Wehrmacht objected to, but which at this time became protection squads for top Nazis. For the specific role of smashing political opposition Himmler formed a number of Political Alarm Squads (*Politische Bereitschaften*). Hard-pressed police chiefs in Bavaria, and outside it, availed themselves of these ruthless gladiators in the Nazi cause.

Goering was at the same time creating the force of political secret police which in time would make all occupied Europe tremble. Known at first as Section 1A, at Goering's command it was swiftly expanded by a young Prussian official named Dr Rudolf Diehls, and given the name of Secret State Police (*Geheime Staatspolizei*).

Goering freed it from the need to abide by the law for the treatment of prisoners and suspects, and under Diehls made it responsible directly to him so that in its task of persecuting non-Nazi Germans it was beyond the law. Goering caused its anti-Bolshevik section to be housed in Berlin's former Communist headquarters, the Karl Liebknecht House. Its official abbreviation – *Gestapa* – was changed by popular use to the more sinister sounding Gestapo.

This rapid transformation of Germany into a police state was accompanied by the preparation of Hitler's Enabling Act, designed deliberately to deliver the *coup de grâce* to parliamentary democracy. It was presented to the Reichstag in the Kroll Opera House in Berlin on 24 March 1933, while outside rank upon rank of armed S.A. and S.S. men barked in chorus: 'We want the Act – or murder and fire.'

Mockingly entitled 'Law for Relieving the Distress of Nation and Reich', it enabled the Chancellor to promulgate laws without the President's consent, to remake the Constitution, decree the Budget, legislate upon any subject – in fact, do anything except alter the present form of the Reichstag, or end the office of the Presidency. No German citizen had any right of appeal against any Government measure under the Act. It was to last initially for four years and was supposed to become void with a change of government.

Left: Stormtroopers enforce the one-day boycott of Jewish businesses at a store in Berlin on 1 April 1933.

Far left: Bodyguards keep a watchful eye on Hitler as he mounts the steps to the podium in the 1933 Nuremberg Rally. Behind him follow Hess, Goebbels and other Nazi leaders.

on their heads and comport themselves with dignity, as though they were making a pleasant excursion by water.'

After the emergency decrees and the Enabling Act, the next logical step was Nazification of every field of national life—*Gleichschaltung*, or 'co-ordination'. It included the States, the municipalities, the civil service, the trade unions, other political parties and in a sense too, anti-Semitism. 'The Party', Hitler told Hermann Rauschning, 'takes over the function of what has been society. The Party is all-embracing. It rules our lives in all their breadth and depth ... There will be no licence, no free space in which the individual belongs to himself.' Such were the oppressive ideas behind Nazification.

The sixteen German federal States, or *Länder*, having been saddled with Nazi Governors, now by order of Interior Minister Wilhelm Frick on 31 March 1933 lost all their sovereign rights to the Berlin Government. Reconstituted to create Nazi majorities, the States' Governments were empowered to annul existing State laws and to legislate in disregard of their Constitutions, being obliged to accept dissolution automatically if the Reichstag was dissolved.

Thus they were in effect transformed into administrative departments of the Nazi Government in Berlin, whose laws and decrees, imposed by the Governors, covered all fields of national life. Most important, control of the police, hitherto a states' right, was now to be transferred to Frick's Ministry of the Interior—excepting Prussia, where Hermann Goering at first hung on to personal control, including especially control of the Gestapo.

But a dramatic increase in power now came to Himmler, whom Frick authorized on his behalf to start taking over control of the states' police. Himmler would achieve this by early 1934 as well as moving towards Cabinet rank as eventual chief of all Germany's police and the S.S.

Towards the end of March the first anti-Semitic laws were passed in Prussia in what was also a Nazification move. Jewish judges, prosecutors and officials in the criminal courts were forthwith deprived of their posts, and Jewish lawyers were in effect prohibited from working for non-Jews. The right of Jewish barristers to practise was based on the proportion of Jews in the German population, so that in Berlin, for example, only 35 out of 2,500 Jewish lawyers could continue to practise. Under the Nazi racial laws, a person was defined as Jewish even if one only of his four grandparents was a Jew.

The reporting in the foreign Press both of this move and of the many atrocities already inflicted on dissidents, Jews especially, infuriated Hitler. It led to these newspaper reports being made the pretended cause of a Jewish boycott day on 1 April 1933. 'Communist and Marxist enemies and their Jewish intellectual instigators who took their money abroad,' said a Nazi manifesto, 'are unloosing from

Presenting it, Hitler promised that the President's powers as well as the rights of the States and the Churches would be untouched and that the powers under the Act would be used only for essential matters; but its rejection would be taken as a declaration of resistance. Peace or war between the Parties, he ended threateningly, depended upon the passage of the Act.

In this atmosphere of intimidation the two-thirds majority was obtained and the Act was passed, while the auditorium and the streets outside echoed to the Nazis' roars of triumph. Only 94 deputies—the Social Democrats—voted against it, the other 26 of them being either forcibly detained or in prison. Many of the 81 Communist deputies were in Oranienburg concentration camp, the rest were excluded from voting. The Catholics, after agonized indecision, voted for the Act, and no prayers ever rescued them from the consequences of that folly.

Chancellor Hitler now had the power which hitherto only the President had possessed, to issue emergency decrees. It was a weapon that, combined with the decree of February ending the liberty of the German subject, put the people totally at his mercy. Why did not Hugenberg, von Papen and the Nationalists withdraw their support from the Nazis in the face of this transformation of Germany's political and social scene far beyond the needs of 'peace and order'? Konrad Heiden has given a succinct answer: 'The flood rose steadily round these men in the German Nationalist Front. All they did was to place their top hats firmly

Members of the Nazi student society, the *Studentschaft*, together with Stormtroopers, trample on a lorry-load of 'un-German' books which they have removed from a university library. Few German academics opposed this enforcement of Nazi cultural doctrine in the universities.

abroad an unscrupulous and treasonable agitation against the German nation.'

Throughout Germany on 1 April, S.A. and S.S. men picketed Jewish-owned stores and shops and threateningly warned off non-Jewish customers. In an atmosphere heavy with menace, Jewish professors and students were excluded from universities, and Jewish professional men and businessmen were isolated from their clients. In a move to silence critical reports abroad, Nazi speakers and newspapers threatened to intensify the boycott and to crush the Jewish people unless the reports ceased. In a letter to Hitler, Hindenburg protested ineffectively about the injustice to Jewish ex-soldiers.

Next to feel the crack of the Nazi whip were Germany's civil servants, one and a half million strong, and hitherto impartial, non-political, incorruptible and reasonably efficient. A new law, entitled with characteristic Nazi hypocrisy 'For the Restoration of the Civil Service', ordered officials not of Aryan descent to be placed on the retired list forthwith, except for those who had lost father or son in the War or who had fought in it themselves. Officials who had obtained their posts on the basis of membership of a political party without possessing the necessary qualifications were dismissed with three months' salary but no pension. The dismissal of anyone believed politically unreliable and those whose departure would improve stability and efficiency was also authorized.

Decreed in spite of a law passed over 50 years before which gave civil servants life appointments in the interests of an efficient service, the new law opened the door to unqualified Nazis, to tyranny and the spread of abuses. Catholics and Social Democrats were flung out to make way for Nazis. So much damage was done that Hitler protested that brains, except when they were non-Aryan brains, had to be the foremost consideration in the service,

whether or not they were Nazi brains. 'Theoretical coordination will not bring the workers their bread,' he declared.

By the end of April, Nazification was spreading its corrosive poison into the schools and universities. Scores of Jewish professors, even those with the highest scientific qualifications, were forced to resign as part of a 'purification campaign'. An internationally famous physicist and holder of the Iron Cross (First Class), Dr James Franck, a Nobel prize winner and head of the Institute for Experimental Physics in Göttingen University, though in view of his background not made to go, nevertheless resigned owing to the prevailing anti-Semitism in academic circles.

At the same time, a Nazi official student organization called the *Studentschaft*, composed of a student Leader and a student Council, made its appearance in German universities. It was authorized to take part in the deliberations of university senates, to cooperate in maintaining order among students, to carry out student self-government, to restrict admission to students of Nazi sympathies and to exclude Marxist, Social Democratic and often even Catholic students.

Studentschaft members led the campaign to apply Nazi cultural doctrine in the universities. On 10 May 1933 Berlin University Nazis swarmed into its libraries, removed some 20,000 volumes of 'un-German' writers and, after an inflammatory speech by Dr Goebbels, transported them to the Opera House square, where–encouraged by professors–they made a vast bonfire of them.

Many books were forbidden on the sole ground that they were by Jewish authors, however esteemed their contents. The 'un-German' authors included Emil Ludwig,

Saluting Nazis burn thousands of volumes of 'un-German' literature in a Berlin square in May 1933.

Ernst Toller, Thomas and Heinrich Mann, Stefan Zweig, Hermann Hesse, H. G. Wells, Henri Barbusse, Sigmund Freud, Romain Rolland and Selma Lagerlöf.

The scene was repeated at famous universities across the whole country. At Frankfort-on-Main the condemned books were brought for burning in ox-drawn manure carts under the approving eye of the university Rector. By 20 May, in Berlin alone, more than 500 tons of 'un-German' books had been destroyed. Signifying the abject and speedy capitulation of the academics, not one university objected, while several professorial voices even praised 'these flames of purification'.

The flames heralded a wave of cultural Nazification. Curators of the four museums in Berlin housing the national art collections, and of others throughout Germany, were dismissed either on racial or political grounds. Orchestral conductors and musicians of the status of Bruno Walter, Otto Klemperer and Artur Schnabel were forbidden to perform in public because their 'conception of their art was contrary to true German character and feeling.'

Albert Einstein, who had already left Germany, now resigned from both the Prussian and the Bavarian Academies of Sciences. The Prussian Academy, he declared, had failed to make any protest against the violation of the rights of those eminent scholars who had been driven out of their appointments and deprived of their livelihood. 'The German public is so cowed by the reign of terror that it has lost all power of resistance,' he lamented.

Nazification spread its tentacles into the Press. Otto Dietrich, Hitler's Press chief, who was at the end of April made director of the Association of the German Press, promptly expelled Jewish, Marxist and Social Democrat journalists, thus preventing them from earning a living in Germany.

The appointment in April of Hans Frank – later Governor-General of Poland – as Minister for Co-ordination of Justice marked the penetration of Nazification into the judicial sphere with the formation of the League of German Jurists and the publication of a new Nazi law code of increased severity, including the more widespread use of the death penalty against criminal offenders.

On 28 April 1933 the faithful Rudolf Hess was rewarded by Hitler for his devotion with his appointment as Deputy Leader of the Party, with authority to deal with issues in the Führer's name. And at the end of this eventful month, with its whirlwind of Nazification, Franz Seldte, chief of the Nationalist *Stahlhelm*, transferred the 250,000 members of this private army *en bloc* to Hitler, who gratefully merged them with the 600,000 S.A. Seldte then left the National Front and joined the Nazis, remaining in the Government as Minister of Labour despite the feeble protests of the unhappy Hugenberg.

Goebbels, who on 31 March 1933 had been taken into the Government as chief of the new Ministry of Public Enlightenment and Propaganda, rejoiced at the speed with which Hitler forced changes through. 'The Leader's personality is now completely in the ascendant in the Cabinet,' he noted gleefully on 22 April. 'There will be no more voting. The Leader decides. Everything has been achieved much more quickly than we had dared to hope.'

The first of May 1933 was celebrated as a new May Day Festival of National Labour. Hitler told a mass meeting that it marked the end of class warfare and a new era for labour. The well-kept secret of the destruction of the 'free', or Social Democrat trade unions next day was therefore a national shock. Under the direction of the bibulous Dr Robert Ley's Factory and Office Cells Organization,

Stormtrooper detachments seized trade union offices, premises, newspapers and banks throughout Germany. Some 50 leading trade unionists, including Herr Lipart, President of the four-million-strong Trade Union Federation, were arrested and thrown into concentration camps, while the Workers' Bank was put under a Nazi Commissioner. At one blow, political trade unionism throughout Germany was destroyed.

A Nazi manifesto declared that National Socialism must represent labour, and referred to the union leaders as 'Red criminals who for generations misused you, good-humoured, honest and upright German workman, in order to dispossess and disinherit you and the whole nation. For this reason, we are taking their main weapon from the hand of the Marxists. Not that we want to destroy the trade unions. No, workman! Your institutions are to us National Socialists sacred and inviolable. We will not only maintain, we will extend the workers' safeguards and rights.'

In one day, the brown shirt was thus forced on the trade unions. Next morning, Robert Ley was appointed leader of the new Nazi Labour Front to be formed from the now defunct Socialist unions. The day after, frightened by the takeover, some 21 other unions 'unconditionally and without reserve' submitted themselves to Hitler's leadership. They included 600,000 members of the Catholic Trade Union Federation, 300,000 of the Employers' Unions and several smaller organizations. Even the powerful Herr Krupp von Bolen toed the line, met Hitler and agreed on 4 May 1933 to Nazi control over the influential League of German Industrialists. Germany's entire force of organized labour and the most influential section of heavy industry thus capitulated to the Nazis almost without protest.

But destruction of the unions was only a half-way house in the political phase of the revolution. On 26 May 1933 the Nazis began a campaign to destroy all Germany's other political parties by confiscating the entire resources of the Communist Party, its leaders being already mostly prisoners in concentration camps.

Hitler then threatened his Cabinet colleague Hugenberg's National Front para-military organizations with a 'bloodbath' at the hands of the more powerful S.A. unless they dissolved or merged with the Nazis. Having failed in his objective, on 21 June he ordered the police and S.A. to seize their property and banned them on the unconvincing ground that there were Communists among them. The protests of Hugenberg, treated as a pariah by the four Nazis—Hitler, Goering, Frick and Goebbels—who dominated the Cabinet, went unheard.

It was next the turn of the once-powerful Social Democrats. On 22 June 1933 Stormtrooper detachments occupied their party and newspaper premises throughout Germany, beat up and arrested their staffs and confiscated their property. As always, the 'ruthless brutality' which Hitler admired marked the action, and during the next few days leading Social Democrats were murdered or seized

and flung into concentration camps. Frick, announcing the suppression of the Social Democrat Party, declared that its leaders were guilty of high treason—they were plotting with former colleagues abroad to overthrow the Government. All 120 of the party's deputies lost their Reichstag seats and numerous Social Democrat officials in Government and municipal departments were dismissed.

Four days later, on 27 June 1933, came the expected end of the National Front. In a letter to President Hindenburg the day before, Hugenberg gave an account of the Nazi conspiracies against him and his party, and asked that his resignation from his two Ministries, Food and Agriculture, and Economics, be accepted, but evidently both this and a later letter to Hindenburg were held back.

At midday on 27 June, during an angry meeting, Hitler threatened that if Hugenberg resigned from the Cabinet many thousands of Nationalist civil servants would lose their posts. He asked him to continue, but with duties of less importance and an agreement that the National Party must cease. Despite these threats, however, Hugenberg resigned. That evening, he and other Nationalist leaders dissolved the Party, believing that worse might happen otherwise; and to forestall violence by the S.A. two of the Party leaders visited Hitler at once and signed an order ending it.

The end of the remaining parties came quickly. The German State (Constitutional) Party, deprived of its Reichstag representation next day, promptly dissolved. On 4 July 1933 the German People's Party and the Bavarian People's Party followed suit.

The sixty-year-old Catholic Centre Party, whose leader Heinrich Brüning had been negotiating with Hitler and Frick about its future, was now the only one surviving. But Nazi intentions were made clear on 1 July 1933 when the Gestapo, without warning, suppressed Catholic organizations with a total of nearly half a million members. Four days later the Party leaders, knowing the future was hopeless, formally announced its end.

On 14 July 1933, the Cabinet passed a law prohibiting the formation of new parties and attempts to keep old ones alive, with penalties of up to three years' imprisonment for offenders. 'There is only one political party in Germany,' it decreed, 'and that is the National Socialist German Workers' Party.'

Political activity apart from the Nazi Party henceforward involved the risk of a painful death in a concentration camp. Democracy among the German people had, owing to historical conditions, a short enough life, and now the Nazis had crushed it underfoot. But their dictatorship was to prove a two-edged weapon, for without the restraint of an Opposition, the Hitlerian madness was to make a vast concentration camp of Germany, where the human mind and spirit as well as bodies were in chains. In this situation lay the seeds of the doom of the Third Reich.

Signs of the virulence of Nazi doctrines had already become clear. The 14 July Cabinet meeting which ended non-Nazi political life also decreed, among some 20 other laws, a law implementing the enforced sterilization of sufferers from hereditary diseases and the establishment of a Hereditary Health Court authorized to adjudicate in this field.

From such thinking grew the plans for the sterilization experiments conducted upon women in Ravensbruck concentration camp, and the wartime centres for euthanasia.

Already, the role of women was looked upon as strictly biological. Another law decreed early in July 1933 stated that up to their 35th year women were candidates for matrimony and therefore were not to be granted permanent salaried status as State or municipal employees or in semi-public institutions. Yet it is fair to say that no obstacles were placed in the way of women of exceptional talent and energy who wanted to fulfil themselves in their chosen trade or profession, always provided that they served the Nazi cause. Two such examples were Leni Riefenstahl, the film producer, and Hanna Reitsch, the woman test pilot and aviator, both of whom were highly regarded by Hitler. Speaking generally, however, Hitler wanted more children for the Hitler Youth and young men for the expanded Reichswehr.

For Hitler had made a bargain with the generals: the assurance of a greatly expanded and re-armed Reichswehr, and no Nazification (as he had outlined to them in a private address when he became Chancellor), in exchange for neutrality during his suppression of the political parties. The Reichswehr, under Defence Minister General von Blomberg, had kept its bargain and shown remarkable restraint, for many officers and men were Catholics and inclined towards the now-defunct Centre Party; and many were Nationalists. A Reichswehr threat of action if these parties were crushed like the Communists would have been by no means unpopular and could well have ended Nazification and started Hitler on a downward path. Hitler never forgot the decisive restraint of the Reichswehr during the days when he was forging his dictatorship over Germany.

Ernst Röhm, however, now chief of the huge S.A., which in July 1933 numbered nearly three million, yearned for a new revolutionary army based on the S.A., and the much smaller Reichswehr, which he would command. Linked with the demand among S.A. leaders and some of the top Nazis for a second revolution, this was to lead to an upheaval in the Party and Hitler's use of S.S. killers in June 1934 to murder hundreds of old Party members.

HITLER'S RIVATE LIFE
Vegetarianism
Cream Cakes and Table Talk

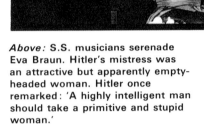

Above: S.S. musicians serenade Eva Braun. Hitler's mistress was an attractive but apparently empty-headed woman. Hitler once remarked: 'A highly intelligent man should take a primitive and stupid woman.'

Right: Hitler dozes under the adoring gaze of his niece, Geli Raubel. The mysterious circumstances of her suicide have never been satisfactorily explained.

Only in the 1920s and 30s did Hitler enjoy a private life. From about mid-1940 onwards he was so occupied with war, as Germany's Supreme Commander, that every moment of his time had inevitably to be sacrificed to it.

Before the War he liked going to bed usually well after midnight because in the evenings and at nights he felt at his best. His most recent biographer, Werner Maser, discloses that he used to wake at 10 a.m. after his customary late night and, wearing one of his favourite nightshirts, would collect the bundle of reports and memoranda from a chair outside his bedroom door and go back to bed to study them.

Then he washed or bathed, shaved (a tremor in his hand in later years made a barber needful) and dressed ready for breakfast at 11 a.m., usually cold milk, an apple and a piece of crispbread. Vegetarianism and abstinence from tobacco and alcohol were features of his entire adult life; guests at the Berghof were careful never to smoke in his presence.

The War changed his daily routine entirely. After a late vegetarian supper in his field headquarters he busied himself with military situation reports until 8 a.m.; he then played briefly with his Alsatian puppy before going to bed for perhaps two hours, after which he resumed work.

His health suffered from this régime; he contracted high blood pressure and a weakened heart, becoming dependent upon the dubious pills and injections prescribed for him by his quack physician Dr Theo Morell. The belief that he was syphilitic is now known to be false. The results now available of three standard tests—Wassermann, Kahn and Meinicke, which his chronic hypochondria drove him to have in 1940, were all negative.

And far from being homosexual—another common misapprehension—he was strongly attracted by and attractive to women after the first inhibitions of his early youth had gone. In Munich in the 1920s he was known for the readiness with which he embarked on affairs with women. Apart from Eva Braun, who came on the scene a bit later, they included his much-loved cousin, Geli Rabaul, with whom he lived in Munich in 1928, and who, owing to this affair, shot herself in 1931; also Inge Ley, a former actress, Susi Liptauer, an Austrian beauty, and even Martha Dodd, daughter of the U.S. Ambassador. Various rich women, including Frau Helene Bechstein, gave him objets d'art and costly pieces of jewellery to help him and his Party survive inflation.

His private entertaining at the Berghof, according to people who visited him often, was entirely commonplace and lacking any cultural impulse. Talk was dominated by the Führer's long rambling monologues. Most memorable were the tea parties and the great quantities of cream cakes which giant young S.S. men persistently offered the guests.

Right: Hitler is seen here on a country ramble with Dr Morell, his personal physician, Bruckner, his adjutant, and the architect Fick.

Below: Hitler, Goebbels and Frau Goebbels are caught in a serious mood during a tea-time discussion.

Röhm and the Bloodbath of 1934

Hitler digs the first spadeful during the construction of the new Reich autobahn in Frankfurt in 1933. It was part of the vast programme of roads, public buildings, barracks and armaments that laid the foundations of Germany's economic recovery in the late 1930s.

For Hitler, the Nazis and Germany, July 1933 marked a turning point in the forward march. Salient features of their policy were by now fully under way—anti-Semitism, terrorism, concentration camps, rearmament, and Nazification of all fields of national life.

Relations with the Roman Catholic Church had been codified in a Concordat signed in Rome in July by von Papen and Cardinal Pacelli, which imposed on German bishops an oath of loyalty to the Reich and forbade priests and lay officials to take part in any non-Nazi political activities. The Protestant Lutheran Church was also involved in a Nazification campaign. Pro-Nazis among its members had evolved the notion of 'German Christians' with the motto of 'One God, One People, One Reich, One Church'. They were 'Christians' who supported anti-Semitism and Nazi racial policy and were led by a former Reichswehr chaplain, Ludwig Müller, who with Hitler's support had been appointed Reich Bishop.

The Nazis saw Christianity as hostile to and incompatible with their own creed, and these were the first steps to try to mould it in the Nazi image. It seemed at first as if they had won the day; but later, Pastor Martin Niemöller and the theologian Dietrich Bonhöffer, among others, launched an opposition which shone brightly even in the darkest days of the Nazi terror.

The vital need for Hitler now was to harness Nazis and people in a fight for economic revival. Despite all the brutality since he came to power, Hitler had touched hidden depths in the German soul; signs of a national awakening existed beyond doubt in late 1933. He determined as a first move to exploit this in a plebiscite. Voters, men and women, were asked, ambiguously: 'Do you approve this policy of your Government, and are you prepared to declare it an expression of your own will and solemnly to acknowledge it as such?'

Out of 43·5 million voters, or 96·3 per cent of the electorate, 40·6 million voted for, and 2·1 million against; 750,000 papers were 'invalid', which amounted to 95·1 per cent for and 4·9 per cent against. Even allowing as much as 20 per cent for rigging and terror, this was a considerable achievement.

A great shout of approval had apparently echoed over Germany—despite methods which in England, France or the United States would have caused violent upheavals. For the Nazis had managed to kill the hitherto prevalent feeling that Germany was the whipped dog of Europe. They had restored national pride and created the belief that the German people were on the march again to their special national destiny. It engendered a heady mood of exhilaration and triumph backed by the unquestioning faith in the

Hitler joins Generals von Blomberg and von Fritsch on
manœuvres. In 1938 both men were dismissed on
charges of immorality. Blomberg had married a woman
who had a police record as a prostitute; Fritsch was
quite falsely accused of homosexuality.

Führer that made them ignore vicious crimes and welcome desperate adventures.

Hitler knew it. 'I will make of Germany an armed camp,' he vowed. He meant a great army, well equipped with tanks, artillery and dive-bombers, of course; but no less he intended a psychological change, through which the entire nation would be galvanized by the alert, intrepid, fanatical, do-or-die spirit of war, so that the Nazi policy of establishing their new world order would be feasible.

A menacing problem, however, stood in Hitler's way. Behind the impressive façade– *'Ein Reich, ein Volk, ein Führer!'* –the Nazi Party was split into two mutually antagonistic factions. The 'Party' faction, led by Frick, Goering, Himmler, his bloodthirsty lieutenant Heydrich, and backed by Hindenburg, von Blomberg and Vice-Chancellor von Papen, sought to end revolutionary activity and develop Nazi Germany in cooperation with bourgeois society as a tightly controlled capitalist economy.

The other force, led by Ernst Röhm and the group of homosexual S.A. leaders surrounding him, and supported at first by Goebbels, sought to absorb the Reichswehr into the S.A. and launch a second revolution. The existing form of society would be destroyed and replaced by National Socialism and an anti-capitalist alliance with Soviet Russia against the West, in which the German eagle would dominate the Russian bear.

It was a conflict of interests which, owing to the lawless violence upon which Nazism was based, could only end in a bloodbath in which murder would be enshrined, tensions in Germany increased and the distraction of war made certain. But in July 1933 Hitler, not yet committed to either side, hoped to heal this split and stop the second revolution idea through his own leadership. 'The revolution is not a permanent state of affairs, and it must not be allowed to develop into such a state,' he told the Reich Commissioners on 6 July 1933. 'The stream of revolution released must be guided into the safe channel of evolution . . . The ideas of the Programme oblige us not to act like fools and upset everything but to realize our trains of thought wisely and carefully.'

Wilhelm Frick sounded another note of warning on 12 July 1933. 'The German revolution is closed,' he declared. 'The National Socialist Party has become the State, and all the power of the State lies in the hands of the Hitler Government, in which all important posts are occupied by reliable Nazis. Therewith the victorious National Revolution has entered on the stage of evolution by normal legal and constructive work. It is the most important function of the Government now to consolidate, both economically and spiritually, the foundations of the power invested in it. In this task, however, the Government will be hampered if there is any more talk of a continuation of the revolution, or of a second revolution. Anyone speaking in this way must realize that he is rebelling against the leader and will be treated accordingly.'

Goering, early in August, took a step towards 'normal legal and constructive work' by ending the powers of the

Top: Röhm attends one of his last Stormtrooper rallies. He is accompanied by Karl Ernst (right).

S.A. auxiliary police and dismissing them. But Röhm, far from being frightened into submission, issued his own challenge to the Party group: 'Anyone,' he told a rally of more than 80,000 Stormtroopers on 6 August, 'who thinks that the tasks of the S.A. have been accomplished will have to get used to the idea that we are here and intend to stay here, come what may.' Earlier, he had threatened that up to 12 members of any organization responsible for the murder of a Stormtrooper would be brought to justice. Was it intended as a warning to the S.S. or the Reichswehr not to lay hands on the S.A.?

Kurt Ludecke, who had been Hitler's special representative in the U.S.A., and whom in May Goering had unjustly thrown into prison, gained a valuable insight into Röhm's mind in the summer of 1933. Discussing the moral cleansing he was about to campaign for in the Party, he told Röhm it might lead to attacks on him for the notorious homosexual groups which flourished around him in the top levels of the S.A.

'I've suffered enough from that,' Röhm replied. 'I'll be free of it—that Damocles sword isn't going to hang over me any longer. Homosexuality isn't a sufficient reason for removing an able and honest leader from any position, so long as he's discreet . . . But to hell with pederasty. I can and will restrain myself if that's the stumbling block. Haven't I worked all my life for this land and given Hitler all I had? Where would he be without me? Hitler had better look out—the German Revolution is only beginning!'

Röhm then launched a massive expansion of the S.A., enrolling men not only from the *Stahlhelm* but also from the banned Communist Red Front para-military organization too. 'Let them call them "beefsteaks",' he told Ludecke, after someone had said they were 'brown' outside but 'red' inside. 'I like them radical. Most of the ones who join us become Nazi revolutionaries and that's what we want. Some of my best men are former Communists.' Before the year's end the numbers of the Stormtroopers would grow to over four million. This fateful problem smouldered during the next 12 months like a threatening volcano while other issues also clouded the horizon.

On 15 November 1933 Dr Goebbels established a Reich Chamber of Culture to which all creative artists and journalists who wished to continue working were forced to belong. Its objects were to ensure the Germanic content of art, music, literature, drama, radio and the Press, as well as to refuse membership to and expel any offending worker in these fields. Creative artists were thus blinkered and muzzled, or silenced.

Tension between Austria and Germany worsened with the outlawing of the Austrian Nazis in August by Chancellor Dollfuss. German broadcasts began insolently to demand new Austrian elections in which the Nazis could take part. Then relations were clouded with hostility when an Austrian Nazi shot and wounded Dollfuss; and a cam-

Bottom: Women press forward to touch Hitler at a harvest festival. The ordinary German regarded Hitler as the leader who had made a reality of their longings for a new and powerful Germany.

paign of sabotage by bombing began as part of Nazi plans for *Anschluss*, or forced union.

Another row blew up at the League of Nations Geneva Disarmament Conference in October 1933. Britain and France strongly opposed Germany's demand for equality of status in armaments and for permission to rearm at once. Hitler immediately declared that Germany could 'no longer participate in the Conference and has decided to notify the League of Nations of the Reich's withdrawal from that body'. Calling the League's attitude 'humiliating and dishonourable', Hitler announced that he would submit the issue to a German plebiscite.

For Hitler a clear national affirmation of his rearmament policy was vital. If international action or public opinion at home hampered it, disappointed Reichswehr generals might end their neutrality towards the Nazis and oppose Hitler's greatest wish – to succeed Hindenburg both as President and as Supreme Commander of the Armed Forces.

The date of both the elections and the plebiscite was fixed for 12 November 1933. A wave of terrorism and propaganda hit the nation like a tornado. When the electorate trooped obediently to the polling booths in November to elect 685 Nazis to the Reichstag and to declare on Government policy, out of 43·4 million plebiscite votes, 40·5 million voted Yes. For the Reichstag candidates, out of 42·9 million, 39·6 million voted Nazi. About 3·3 million papers were spoiled by courageous objectors.

Significantly, Hitler gave public thanks to Dr Goebbels' Propaganda Department, to the Stormtroopers, to the Press and to Heinrich Himmler's Political Defence Squads for having achieved 'prodigies, in just under three weeks'. More than ever, Hitler seemed dependent upon the S.A. as the Party's apparatus of coercion, for there can be little doubt that one way or the other the voting was rigged.

A settlement with Röhm and the S.A. now became vital, for in face of the withdrawal from the League and the manipulated vote at home in support of the rearmament policy, France had come out with a strong call for a united front of European powers against Germany. For this reason, and to ease the threat of the columns of Stormtroopers aching for revolution, Hitler made their Chief of Staff Röhm – and Hess too, for different reasons – Ministers without Portfolio in the Cabinet. Röhm was angry, not appeased; determined, not dissuaded – for Goering of all men had been appointed a general of the Reichswehr and Hitler had promised General von Blomberg a Field-Marshal's baton if he became President. Nor was Röhm deceived or pacified by Hitler's warmly phrased letter to him of 2 January 1934 emphasizing the separate roles of Reichswehr and S.A.

Published in the *Völkischer Beobachter*, the letter stated that the National Socialist revolution was 'only made possible by the wholesale suppression of the Marxist terror by the S.A. If the Reichswehr must guarantee the protection of the nation externally, then it is the task of the S.A. to guarantee internally the victory of the National Socialist State . . .

'When I appointed you, my dear Chief of Staff . . . the S.A. was going through a grave crisis. Above all it is due

to you that within a few years this political instrument has been able to develop that force which by overcoming the Marxist opposition made it possible for me to win decisively in the struggle for power. Hence . . . my dear Ernst Röhm, I feel the urge to thank you for the imperishable services you have rendered the National Socialist movement and the German people, and to assure you how grateful I am to destiny for being allowed to number such men as you among my friends and comrades-in-arms. In cordial friendship and grateful appreciation, Your Adolf Hitler.'

Was this seemingly affectionate letter really a plea to Röhm not to shatter their friendship by challenging Hitler's direction of Nazi policy through trying to take over the function of the Reichswehr in the State? Röhm may well have seen it in this way, for from this time on his role in this conflict and, as a result, that of all those involved except Hitler's, sharpened and hardened irrevocably. Hitler still sought to reconcile and unite.

Rudolf Hess, whose solo flight to Scotland in May 1941, on an abortive peace mission, caused a brief sensation. Sentenced to life imprisonment at Nuremberg, he is still a prisoner in Spandau.

Often this role was forced on him by the power struggles that continued unendingly among his main henchmen. Behind the Party's monolithic façade hatred and envy were rampant as, like Röhm, all of them tried to increase their personal empires at the expense of another – Goebbels versus Goering, Goering versus Ley, Hess versus Himmler, and Himmler silently pitted against them all as was Bormann, when he succeeded Hess as head of the Party Chancellery. Only Hitler, above this constant struggle for power, went unchallenged.

In February 1934, Röhm brought his conflict with the Reichswehr to a head by presenting the new C.-in-C., General Werner von Fritsch, with a memorandum urging in effect that, in a fundamental reversal of roles, the S.A. should take over national defence and the Reichswehr should assume the subordinate function of a training and reinforcement army, both of which should be administered by Röhm as Cabinet member responsible for the armed forces.

This was the dream of a new 'people's army' he had already explained to Hermann Rauschning, the Danzig Nazi leader. 'You won't make a revolutionary army out of the old Prussian N.C.O.s,' he had told Rauschning. 'I'm the nucleus of the new army, don't you see that? Don't you understand that what's coming must be new, fresh and unused? The basis must be revolutionary. You can't inflate it afterwards. You only get the opportunity once to make something new and big that'll help us to lift the world off its hinges.'

Röhm could barely restrain his impatience to explode revolutionary warfare in Germany. Control of the armed forces was a necessary step, but the hope that von Fritsch and the General Staff, with their rigid military etiquette and punctilious regard for protocol, would bow to direction from Colonel Röhm and his wild gang of homosexual S.A. leaders seemed incredible, despite the four million Stormtroopers. Especially offensive to them was the S.A. leaders' arrogant lack of discretion. It had, for example, become widely known that Edmund Heines, Röhm's S.A. deputy in

Adopting a pose of studied informality, Hitler addresses colleagues in the Chancellery. The impassive Bormann listens with studious attention.

Hitler and Röhm take the stage together at an S.A. rally in Nuremberg. By early 1934 the rift between them was widening and Röhm was referring publicly to Hitler as a 'ridiculous corporal'.

Silesia, and Police President of Breslau, had openly set up a group of agents entrusted with the task of finding suitable youths for Röhm's, his own and other leaders' homosexual pleasure. It was too much for the generals' conventional morality.

General von Blomberg put the issue of the Reichswehr's relationship with the S.A. both to Hindenburg and to Hitler. Both rejected Röhm's proposal. But friction with von Blomberg over Röhm's ambitions worsened to the extent that it began to jeopardize his and his fellow generals' faith in Hitler's control over the S.A.; and this was made known to him.

Still desperately pushing his policy of reconciliation, Hitler summoned Reichswehr and S.A. chiefs—von Blomberg, von Fritsch, Röhm, Heines and others—to a meeting where, in his presence, it was plainly laid down and agreed that the Reichswehr's role was to be external operations, and the S.A.'s military training. But no sooner had the generals departed after luncheon that day than the crestfallen Röhm, who had taken much wine, loudly denounced Hitler as a ridiculous corporal and a traitor. Röhm had been thwarted, but not checked.

Goering joined those who feared or opposed Röhm's power and ambition. His Police Presidents in Prussia, largely S.A. men and therefore Röhm's agents, seemed to him a challenge to his control, a threat to his very existence. Therefore, perhaps after a hint from Hitler, he engineered a pact with Himmler, Röhm's comrade from the early days of the Party, who so far had remained loyal to him.

Goering had in February opposed the attempt of Wilhelm Frick and *Reichsführer-S.S.* Himmler to extend Himmler's control of the ordinary police and the political police in other States to Prussia. But in return now for Goering's surrender to him of the Gestapo and the Prussian Police, Himmler secretly agreed on 10 April 1934 to break with Röhm and make an alliance with Goering.

Himmler became chief of the Gestapo, with the title of Inspector. Reinhardt Heydrich, chief of S.S. Security and S.S. Intelligence, became under him, head of the Gestapo. Goering's friend *S.S.-Gruppenführer* Kurt Daluege, a huge one-time S.A. street fighter, whom Goering had made chief of the Prussian Police with the rank of Lieutenant-General, conveniently became chief of all departments of Germany's uniformed police.

The arrangement was another landmark in Himmler's career. Henceforward, with his increased powers, he was to show his true character. He set up his headquarters in the Gestapo building in Berlin's Prinz Albrechtstrasse; while Heydrich moved to the Wilhelmstrasse, in the Security Headquarters of the *Reichsführer-S.S.*

The line-up against Röhm was hardening, but without his knowing. *S.A.-Gruppenführer* Viktor Lutze, loyal before all else to the Führer, had been so shocked to hear Röhm name Hitler 'a traitor' after the meeting to try to smooth over the S.A.'s differences with the Reichswehr, that he informed first Hess and then Hitler himself. Recognizing a man upon whom he could rely in a crisis, Hitler merely thanked him, with the cautious remark: 'We must let the matter develop.'

It came to the ears of Heydrich, who had already made up his mind and was making plans in his cold and deadly way to eliminate not only Röhm but also Heines and most of the other S.A. leaders surrounding him. Having regard to Nazism's violent background, this meant murder.

But S.S. spies could find no evidence that Röhm was planning an uprising, nor even anything to justify an arrest and a charge of treason. Whatever plans for this Röhm had made he kept secret for the time being. Heydrich therefore gave his mind to the task of inventing a charge, at the same time making a list of those who might have to die when the crunch came.

In mid-April Hitler had still apparently not made up his mind which side to back, although the news that Hindenburg might not live more than another three or four months added urgency to the need for a settlement that would gratify the Reichswehr generals. There is no direct evidence to support the story that Hitler, reviewing the German fleet in the Baltic on board the pocket-battleship *Deutschland* with von Blomberg, made a pact to check Röhm and the S.A. if von Blomberg and the Reichswehr would support his succession to the Presidency. But it would be extraordinary if the two men did not reach some sort of understanding of this kind, so vital for both of them.

Afterwards, the hesitation which had marked Hitler's attitude to the issue seemed to vanish. Immediately on his return he renewed his offer to Britain and France in the disarmament negotiations to set in hand a massive decrease in the S.A. to about 750,000. It was an attractive way of weakening the S.A., but not of disarming; he had already ordered von Fritsch to prepare to increase the Reichswehr threefold to 300,000. But it represented a threat to Röhm.

On 27 April 1934 an official communiqué told the nation of the serious decline in President Hindenburg's health, and speculation as to his successor grew feverish. Settlement with Röhm thus became imperative, for there were two other presidential candidates beside Hitler—his old friend General Ritter von Epp, and the German Crown Prince, *S.A.-Gruppenführer* Prince August Wilhelm of Prussia.

Von Blomberg—as part of the *Deutschland* agreement?—rebuffed the monarchists who favoured the Crown Prince by parading the Reichswehr bond of fraternity with the Party through an order stating that from 1 May 1934 all officers and men would wear the Nazi swastika and eagle on their caps and uniforms as a symbol of their loyalty. Admiral Raeder ordered Navy personnel to do the same. Hitler thus gained a great psychological victory, because in a sense the Army was now committed to Nazism and all it stood for. Soon this was to be openly recognized.

First, however, on 16 May 1934, according to one report quoted by the historian Sir John Wheeler-Bennett, the Reichswehr's senior generals met to decide who should be their Supreme Commander on Hindenburg's death. According to this report, Hitler was only the third choice, but von Blomberg's revelation of the *Deutschland* agreement turned the tide immediately. Chancellor Adolf Hitler was accepted by all.

On 25 May came confirmation of von Blomberg and von Fritsch's allegiance in the publication of an updated version of the troops' official handbook, *Duties of the German Soldier*. It stated that 'Military service is a service of honour to the German *Volk*' instead of the former declaration of independence of political parties. The *Volk* was, in effect, the Nazi Party, the Party was the State, and the Reichswehr had lost its independence.

Von Blomberg seems to have been fulfilling the terms of a bargain. Hitler, in turn, now moved again to check Röhm and the S.A. This was rendered urgent through reports reaching him from Himmler and Heydrich that Röhm was involved with General von Schleicher, the former Chancellor, in a plot for a putsch against the Government, with the aim of replacing it by one including themselves, Gregor Strasser and Heinrich Brüning. Afterwards, the Reichswehr would be used to support a second revolution to overthrow capitalism.

On 4 June 1934 Hitler abruptly summoned Röhm to an immediate meeting with him in the Chancellery. For five hours, behind the closed doors of Hitler's private office, the two old friends argued. We have only Hitler's word for what was said – that he told Röhm he had heard of the putsch report; that anyone who attacked the State was his enemy; that he implored Röhm to use his powers to avoid a catastrophe, and reproached him over the scandals associated with his private life.

The outcome was a temporary truce until after Hitler returned from his meeting in Italy with Benito Mussolini in mid-June. In agreement with Röhm, he announced on 8 June 1934 that the S.A. would go on leave for the month of July, when the Stormtroopers would not wear uniforms, demonstrate or take part in military training.

Röhm then let it be known that he was going on sick leave to the lakeside resort of Wiessee, south of Munich. 'If the foes of the S.A. are nursing the hope that the S.A. will not return from their leave or that a part only will return we are ready to let them enjoy this hope for a short time,' he said in a Press announcement that ended: 'At the hour and in the form which appears to be necessary they shall receive the fitting answer. The S.A. is, and remains, Germany's destiny.' It was a defiant way to announce a truce.

This truce, and the forthcoming departure of the S.A. on leave, drove Heydrich, if not his chief Himmler, into a cold fury. The long list of victims destined for murder was ready; the killer squads had been assembled – some of them guards from the Dachau concentration camp; transport, weapons and ammunition had been provided through the good graces of General von Reichenau, chief of the Reichswehr Political Administration Department, and the main accomplice in the anti-Röhm operation. The preliminary moves in the final confrontation had now been made.

Now, at the eleventh hour, despite Himmler's and Heydrich's reports of an imminent S.A. putsch against him, Hitler still hesitated and refused to give the word for the S.S. killers to mow down these old comrades – as well as a number of the *Reaktion* – before he departed for his meeting with Mussolini in Venice on 15 June 1934.

Hitler returned in an ugly mood from Italy – where Mussolini had gone out of his way to treat him as an inferior – to attend a party conference in the town of Gera, near the Czechoslovakian border. While he was there an event occurred that jolted him out of his uncertainty. Hardly had the conference begun when reports began coming in of a speech by Vice-Chancellor Franz von Papen, ringing with an unmistakable counter-revolutionary tone. The fact that it was von Papen, who enjoyed an affectionate, father–son relationship with the ailing Hindenburg, gave the speech even more significance.

'Great men are not made by propaganda, but grow out of their deeds and are recognized by history,' von Papen bluntly told the students of Marburg University, in what seemed a jibe at the Chancellor. And in a direct attack on Hitler's dictatorship: 'The belief that people should be united by terror should be rejected.' He went on to denounce 'all the selfishness, want of principle, untruthfulness, unchivalrous conduct and arrogance that stalks abroad under the cloak of the German revolution. The Government does not fail to recognize that the rich treasure of conscience which the German people give it is threatened. A disfranchised people has no confidence to give,' he added, in an attack on the one-party system.

Roundly he condemned the idea of a second revolution. 'Whoever toys irresponsibly with such ideas should not forget that a second wave might be followed by a third, and that he who threatens to employ a guillotine may be its first victim. Nor is it clear where a second wave is to lead. There is much talk of the coming socialization. Have we gone through the anti-Marxist revolution in order to carry out a Marxist programme? . . . It is time to join together in fraternal friendship and respect for all our fellow countrymen, to avoid disturbing the labours of serious men and to silence fanatics.'

Von Papen had not only condemned present policies, but had brought into the light of day the conflict between the so-called reactionary elements in the Party, who wanted a return to normal conditions, and the fanatical revolutionaries. It was an issue that Hitler could no longer escape. He made a violent attack on von Papen in his speech at Gera: 'It is laughable when such a little worm tries to struggle against so mighty a renewal of a whole people. It is laughable when such a little pygmy imagines he can stop with a few phrases the gigantic renewal of the people's life,' for the benefit of those whom Goebbels' ban on the speech did not prevent from hearing or reading it.

Dr Edgar Jung, a Catholic journalist and one of von Papen's advisers, had prepared the speech weeks earlier; Erich Klausener, leader of the Catholic Action, as well as Baron Fritz-Günther von Tschirschky und Boegendorff, and von Bose and von Dettin, his secretaries, had helped to edit it. All of them had to persuade the frightened von Papen to deliver it, and paid dearly for their trouble.

Von Papen reacted strongly to Goebbels' ban on broadcasts and Press publication of the speech. He went to see Hitler, told him that he had spoken as the President's trustee in what had become a critical situation and that Goebbels' ban would force his resignation.

Top: Stormtrooper standard-bearers hold aloft a forest of banners during the 'Day of the S.S. and the S.A.' at the Nuremberg Rally of September 1934. The banners bear the name of the town or district of each contingent.

Bottom, left: Hitler greets a Stormtrooper leader with the Nazi salute during the 1933 Nuremberg Rally. The occasion was the presentation of standards to new formations.

Hitler confers with Admiral Erich Raeder, C.-in-C. of the German Navy. Raeder carried out Defence Minister von Blomberg's order which instructed all officers and men to wear the Nazi swastika and eagle badge on their caps from 1 May 1934. Nazism thus strengthened its hold over the armed forces.

To have accepted the resignation would have been an admission on Hitler's part that the split between the two factions in the nation was irreparable, and would have provoked a confrontation with Hindenburg. Hitler therefore asked von Papen to withhold his resignation until the two of them had seen the President together, and von Papen agreed.

Hitler now needed Hindenburg's approval for an all-Nazi Cabinet. He therefore broke his agreement with von Papen and flew to Neudeck in East Prussia next day, ostensibly to tell Hindenburg about his meeting with Mussolini, but also to assess the state of the President's health, upon which depended the question of time and to find out the strength of his backing for von Papen.

Reinhardt Heydrich, who was engaged by Himmler in June 1931 to set up a security police organization, the S.D., within the Nazi Party. He is seen here in fencing kit.

He was met formally on the steps of Hindenburg's country house by an unsmiling General von Blomberg who, in a brief but electrifying interview there in the hot sunshine, told him that having been informed of events by Vice-Chancellor von Papen, the President had instructed him to tell the Chancellor that either the Government must bring about a complete relaxation of tension, without any ministerial crisis, or power would be handed over to the Reichswehr and martial law proclaimed. When Hitler insisted, Hindenburg gruffly confirmed this in a four-minute interview.

All too soon, after this brusque reception, Hitler was flying back to Berlin with a crisis on his hands involving his Government's very existence. He was at the crossroads. Either he combined with Röhm and used the S.A. to overthrow the *Reaktion* — Hindenburg, Blomberg, Neurath, von Papen, Schacht and the industrialists' representative Thyssen — even though it meant conflict with the Reichswehr and the elimination of Goering; or he smashed Röhm and the S.A. leaders, secured the confidence of the Reichswehr and the *Reaktion*, and won the Presidency.

He seemingly did not make up his mind for the next two or three days, though Goering and Himmler went on independently with their plans for a purge, adding to their lists old enemies, men who knew too much and even those who were simply regarded as 'dangerous'. But Hitler had his close associates warn both *Reaktion* and revolutionaries about 'trouble-making'. Goebbels attacked 'armchair critics and reactionaries, who would be better under lock and key,' and shouted that, 'While we have destroyed Marxism, we still tolerate reaction.'

Goering, in a speech to the Prussian State Council, had already threatened Röhm and the S.A.: 'It is not our business to determine whether a second revolution is necessary,' he said. 'The first revolution was ordered by the Führer and ended by the Führer. If the Führer wants a second revolution, we shall be ready in the streets tomorrow; if he does not want it we shall crush anybody who wants to make one against the Führer's will.'

Hess, still reflecting Hitler's divided mind, warned the nation on 25 June 1934 against 'malcontents and critics who are sowing discord and distrust among the German people for their own political purposes'. But at the same time he rebuked those who wanted a second revolution. And Goebbels again declared in a speech broadcast throughout Germany that 'the enemy of National Socialism is not to be found among the workers, but among the gentlemen who regard it as a passing phase'. Thus both *Reaktion* and revolutionaries were threatened in this uncertain period.

That day, Monday, 25 June 1934, began ominously the week that would end as one of the most murderous in German history. General von Fritsch, in a move justified only by a grave national emergency, cancelled Army leave, confined officers and men to barracks until further notice and proclaimed an alert. It could have been a precaution against an S.A. putsch.

The Reichswehr now spurned Röhm, who was taking his relaxed cure between the pines and the lakeside at Wiessee, about 40 miles south of Munich. It threw him out of the National Association of German Officers for unbecoming behaviour, behaviour then by no means rare among German officers.

It was an insult with the grimmest implications, which Hitler himself must have authorized. It meant that henceforward Röhm was stigmatized — an outsider, a renegade, unable to look for help even to his officer friends.

That same day came more straws in the wind. The London *News Chronicle* published an interview with Hitler in which the Führer hinted at an approaching crisis and predicted that it could mean sacrificing friends 'of the first hour'. And the respected Swiss *National Zeitung* of Basle published a report that Hitler had decided in view of Hindenburg's declining health to eliminate 'national Bolsheviks'. It said that laws were already being drawn up enabling Hitler to become both Chancellor and President.

Opposite, top: Benito Mussolini, Fascist dictator of Italy. Mussolini treated Hitler disdainfully at their Venice meeting in June 1934 and sent him home in a vengeful mood.

Opposite, bottom: Hitler and Goebbels attend opera at La Scala in November 1933. Although a supposedly passionate lover of opera, Hitler's tastes stretched little farther than Wagner.

Incredibly, *The Times* reporter in Berlin, normally well informed, failed at this time to latch on to any of the facts of the developing crisis.

Meanwhile, the genuine, secret putschists – Goering, Himmler and Heydrich – desperately plotting a coup against Röhm and the S.A. in which Hitler was to be the unknowing tool, from hour to hour 'discovered' fresh evidence, which they fed to the Reichswehr generals as well as Hitler – evidence justifying the belief that an S.A. rising against the Reichswehr was imminent.

A number of the generals, seasoned operators in the sphere of swift mobilization, looked hard but failed to see any signs of such action impending among the S.A. in their districts. Heinz Höhne, the German journalist and author, reports in his recent book that General Ewald von Kleist, doubtful about the information he was receiving about the S.A.'s plans, called for Röhm's intimate Edmund Heines, head of the Silesian S.A., and demanded what was afoot. Heines swore that the S.A. had 'never even dreamt of taking action against the Reichswehr'.

Wondering whether Himmler was not now deliberately trying to engineer a clash between the Army and the S.A., von Kleist spoke to General von Fritsch, who called for General von Reichenau and put the issue to him. Imperturbably, von Reichenau declared: 'That may be, but it's too late now.'

Hitler flew to Essen with Goering on 28 June 1934 to attend the wedding of Josef Terboven, Gauleiter of Westphalia. Listening to Wagner's music and the Nazified wedding service in the old church, he must have thought of murder – to kill or not to kill his old friend, Ernst Röhm, and many other old comrades? For even then, he had not yet decided precisely what course of action to take.

But a telephone message from Himmler, with fresh evidence of distribution of arms to the S.A., so angered him that he left the wedding reception later and returned to his room at the Kaiserhof Hotel with Goering, his adjutant Wilhelm Brückner and others. They were joined by one of Goering's aides from Berlin with more information of S.A. preparations, discovered by the tireless Himmler.

Already, with Himmler manipulating him for his own ends for days, Hitler was strung up nearly to breaking point. Now his control snapped. 'I've had enough,' he shouted. 'I shall make an example of them.' He instructed Goering to return to Berlin at once and await a code word from him to let loose the execution squads. At the same time he ordered a telegram – quoted by Otto Strasser, who does not, however, give the date and place of origin – to be sent to all S.A. headquarters. It said: 'All *Obergruppen-* and *Gruppenführer* are ordered to appear in the staff quarters of the Chief of Staff in Wiessee at 10 a.m. on 30 June. ADOLF HITLER.'

During the afternoon of 29 June 1934 he arrived at the Hotel Dreesen at Bad Godesberg, on the Rhine, having inspected a labour camp in the region. There he ordered Sepp Dietrich, commandant of the *Leibstandarte-Adolf Hitler*, to take two fully armed companies of these bodyguards and go at once to Bad Wiessee, where Röhm was still on leave.

Later, when joined by Goebbels, he received 'information' about S.A. preparedness that prompted him to fly at 2 a.m. to Munich – to which city he also recalled Dietrich and his men – in the belief that the S.A. were to rise at any moment. In fact, most of them were already on leave and Röhm had spent the day relaxing among bronzed young men beside the lake at Wiessee without even troubling to bring his bodyguards from Munich.

In Berlin, Goering assumed emergency powers, Himmler's S.S. were on the streets with machine-guns and Heydrich's execution squads were ready. Von Papen, informed that his collaborator, the Catholic leader Edgar Jung, and his secretaries had been arrested, went to see Goering, whom he found in his study at the Air Transport Ministry with Himmler. Goering told him that Hitler had flown to Munich to deal with S.A. insurgents there and he himself had full powers in Berlin.

Von Papen argued vehemently but vainly that as the Chancellor's deputy these powers belonged by right to him. He then drove to the Vice-Chancellery, where he found that his secretary, Herbert von Bose, had been shot and that the S.S. had occupied his offices. He went home, to be received by a police captain, who said that until further notice he was to be held incommunicado.

The bloodbath was beginning. Hitler had touched down at Munich just after dawn. At the Ministry of the Interior he summoned Munich *S.A.-Obergruppenführer* and Police President August Scheidhuber, and Wilhelm Schmid, *S.A.-Gruppenführer*. Before they could say a word, he cursed them as traitors and shouted that they were under arrest and were to be shot.

He then sped south to Wiessee in a convoy of cars and lorries and with an escort of two armoured fighting vehicles and invaded the Pension Hanselbauer. With a revolver in his hand he pounded on Röhm's door. 'It's I, Hitler, open the door at once!'

Protesting that he didn't expect him till midday, Röhm, who was in bed with Count Hans Joachim von Spreti, unlocked the door. Hitler shouted that he was a traitor and was under arrest, and ordered him and von Spreti to dress at once. Edmund Heines, Police President of Breslau, in the room opposite and in bed with a young S.A. man, was also arrested. All of them were taken to Munich's Stadelheim prison, where they were joined by other S.A. leaders due to be butchered.

Later that day Sepp Dietrich was given a list of the names of 19 of them and ordered to have them shot for high treason. The order came to the ears of Hans Frank, the Nazi legal authority, who refused to allow it until, eventually, he received from Hitler over the telephone the angry assertion that it was a Reich matter which did not concern him.

Before the shooting an S.S. officer told each man: 'The Führer and Reich Chancellor has condemned you to death. The sentence will be carried out forthwith. Heil Hitler!' Protests went unheard. The order to fire was given and the victims crumpled against the prison's grey walls. They included, apart from Heines and von Spreti, several of Hitler's comrades from the struggles of the early days, but

The wedding of *S.A.-Gruppenführer* Karl Ernst. Goering follows the bride and groom with a sinister smile. Ernst was one of the victims of the purge of June 1934.

Röhm was not among them. Hitler could not yet bring himself to order the death without trial of this friend who more than anyone else had helped him to achieve power.

That same day in Bavaria 73-year-old Ritter von Kahr, who had stopped the Munich beer-cellar putsch, was dragged from his home. S.S. killers beat him to death in a swamp near Dachau, where his body was found some days later. The Catholic priest Father Bernhard Stempfle, who had edited *Mein Kampf* and earned Hitler's hatred for this favour, was shot three times in the heart.

In Berlin, Goering had received the code word for action throughout the rest of Germany at about 10 a.m. on 30 June 1934. The list of victims held other names besides those of S.A. leaders – almost anyone who had incurred his or Himmler's or Heydrich's enmity and therefore ranked as an enemy of the State, for revenge was now the password. Several Action Commandos from the *Leibstandarte-Adolf Hitler* were detailed to carry out the murders, some of them in the homes of victims and others in the Lichterfelde barracks. Von Papen's collaborator, Edgar Jung, had already been shot.

One of the first to die was Erich Klausener, a senior civil servant and Catholic Action leader. An S.S. man named Kurt Gildisch shot him in the back of the head in his office without warning. Gregor Strasser, merely rumoured

to have been one of those chosen for the alternative government, was lunching with his wife and children when he was taken away by the Gestapo, flung into their prison in the Prinz Albrechtstrasse and shot down in his cell by Heydrich 12 hours later.

Von Schleicher, the former Chancellor, was sitting at his desk at home when six S.S. killers forced their way in and opened fire. Schleicher fired back, his wife rushed in and was hit in the fusillade as von Schleicher fell dead. General Kurt von Bredow, his assistant, later refused shelter at the house of a foreign diplomat, went home expecting his end and was gunned down at midnight when he answered the ringing of his front-door bell.

In a typical murder for revenge, Erich von dem Bach-Zelewski, an S.S. district commander who rose to the rank of general during the Second World War and crushed the Polish Uprising of 1944, had S.S. killers murder Anton von Hohberg, an S.S. cavalry leader, at his country home. 'We have shot your father,' they told his teenage son, who rushed into the house. They then drove off. These were only the first of a host of murders that day.

Hitler returned to a tense and frightened Berlin at sunset – 'pale, unshaven, sleepless, at once gaunt and puffed' – to be met by Goering and Himmler. Against a blood-red sky, he scanned the list of those whom the executioners had sent to their doom. There were many more to die yet and the shootings went on all next day, a Sunday, as frightened men and women wondered who had survived and whose turn it would be next.

Ernst Röhm was still alive on Sunday afternoon. Hitler told Goering and Himmler that he had pardoned him because of his past services to the Party. This represented a grave danger to both of them, especially Himmler, who had plans to make the S.S., instead of the S.A., supreme in Germany. Nobody knows what was said, but Hitler gave way to their persuasion.

Hitler's last gesture to his old friend was to order that he should be given a revolver and one bullet so that he could kill himself, but Röhm refused to let him escape the responsibility for his murder. Ten minutes later Theodore Eicke and another S.S. man returned and shot him. He died on the floor of his cell at Stadelheim, while Hitler gave a tea party in the Chancellery.

How many had been shot or beaten to death by the time the shooting stopped in the early hours of 2 July 1934? Josef Goebbels refused to permit the publication of obituary notices in the newspapers, and on Hitler's orders all records about the event were destroyed, so only estimates were possible. Gerald Reitlinger quotes the German writer Walter Pechel's figure of 922, including 28 women, which is the highest, others varying from 90 to about 200. Reitlinger also says that about 80 *Leibstandarte* men took an active part in the shootings, which would support the belief in a large number of deaths.

Did Hitler feel safer after the carnage was over and those 'old fighters' of the Party were reduced to ashes in carefully numbered urns? He knew that he had acted illegally and needed immediate protection, for at once on Monday, 2 July, Wilhelm Frick, Minister of the Interior, and the Justice Minister, Franz Gürtner, decreed a law on his behalf legalizing the murders, after the event, 'by the right of the legitimate defence of the State'. Gürtner declared that the purge was 'a statesmanlike duty'.

On behalf of the Reichswehr generals, for whose benefit the S.A. leaders had been shot, von Blomberg praised Hitler's 'soldierly decision' and 'exemplary courage' in destroying 'traitors and mutineers'. If it occurred to him at the time that it had been stupid for the Reichswehr to relinquish its role of protecting the State to the S.S., he did not reveal it. Hindenburg, in a telegram of thanks obviously composed for him, referred to Hitler's 'gallant personal intervention', which had saved the nation from serious danger.

Hitler promoted the S.S. cut-throats who had shown zeal and ability as executioners, and then waited for nearly two weeks before making a public explanation of the massacre. In an attempt to justify it he said that Röhm had promoted a plot with the aid of about £1 million which he had taken from welfare funds to overthrow the present Government. While he himself took charge in Munich, Goering, he said,

had received orders from him to take similar action in Prussia, and 'with an iron fist he beat down the attack on the National Socialist State before it developed'.

Explaining the severity of his countermeasures, he declared: 'Leniency could not exist in this hour. Mutinies are broken by iron laws which are eternally the same. If anyone raises the charge against me that I did not use the ordinary courts for sentencing, I can only say that in this hour I was responsible for the fate of the German nation and that I myself was the supreme court of the German people for this 24 hours.'

Taking the responsibility for all the murders, he went on: 'I gave the order to shoot those who were mainly guilty of this treason and I furthermore gave the order to burn out the tumours of our inner poisoning down to the raw flesh . . .'

He ended with a threat: 'Anyone will know in future that if he lifts his hand against the State certain death is his fate.' The Reichstag Nazis, led by Goering, rose to their feet and cheered, expressed their thanks to Hitler and ended the proceedings by singing the Horst Wessel song.

Thus a song and a cheer brought the curtain down on the most atrocious act so far of the Nazi drama – what might be called the massacre of the summer solstice. Four consequences marked it as an important turning point in the Nazi revolution.

First, the purge had established Hitler as Germany's supreme judge, with the right to send to his death without trial anyone whom he or any of his minions marked as an enemy of the régime. The rule of law, the foundation of civilized life, had been brutally thrust aside. Those whose first duty it was to do so, the representatives of German justice, had not a word of condemnation for this barbarity. As the American historian Eliot B. Wheaton points out, some actually praised it. 'Only one person can determine the laws of the new order, namely the Führer, to whom, through the trust of the people, all authority for creating the new order has been given,' declared one of Germany's most respected legal journals.

Secondly, the S.S. now reached a new level of power and importance, with the prospect of even more as the new guardian of the State – a role which von Blomberg on the Army's behalf had abdicated.

Thirdly, the Army generals, many of whom believed they had called the tune to which Hitler had danced, were now to discover that they were to dance to Hitler's tune, a measure which they were ill equipped to tread.

Fourthly, having finally repudiated National Socialism and the social and economic revolution some of its leaders once called for, Hitler turned instead to expanding Germany's borders by means of reactionary Pan-Germanism, violence and war. Austria was to be the first of his victims.

Opposite, top: General Kurt von Schleicher and his wife; both of them were victims of the S.S. assassination squads on 30 June 1934.

Opposite, bottom: Viktor Lutze, Röhm's successor, leaves Goering's offices in Berlin after his appointment. After the June purge the S.A. never again played an important or independent role in Nazi Germany.

Hitler Youth

Thrills, participation and sense of importance as never before, with gliding, yachting, camping and sports—these and much more the Nazis gave youth in the *Hitlerjugend*. In return they demanded obedience, discipline, self-sacrifice and endurance in the service of National Socialism. 'This new Reich will give its youth to no one, but will itself take youth and give to youth its own education and its own upbringing,' Hitler told a youth mass meeting.

He was telling Germany that the Hitler Youth was the only youth organization allowed. And thus it happened, for although six years after the Hitler Youth was formed in 1926 its membership of boys and girls had reached a mere 35,000, by the end of 1934 membership had grown to six millions. During the previous four years Germany's many other youth organizations—Catholic, Protestant, Communist and Social Democrat to name only four—had been dissolved and their members drawn into the Hitler Youth under the Reich leadership of Baldur von Schirach.

Membership was not compulsory until the outbreak of war in 1939, but a law of 1936 decreed that the entire German youth, apart from its education within the home and in school, was to be educated physically, mentally and morally in the spirit of National Socialism for the service of Germany. Marching boys wore knapsack, blanket-roll, belt and dagger.

So great was the pride of boys and girls in belonging to this prestigious organization that few indeed wished not to join. Apart from the main section in which the chief activities were camping, marching, sport, physical training, Nazi indoctrination and singing in choirs, there were three specialized sections: the Navy (45,000 boys) giving sailing, rowing and nautical training; Flight (55,000 boys) giving gliding and basic navigation training; and Motor (60,000 boys) giving motorbike and car driving, and maintenance.

Training was on the whole pre-military rather than military, and von Schirach trained his own youthful instructors in preference to accepting army officers; nevertheless much importance was given to small-bore rifle shooting. A training document exhibited at the Nuremberg trials declared: 'All training culminates in rifle training. It can scarcely be emphasized enough; and because shooting is a matter of practice, one cannot start too early. The result we want to achieve in the course of time is that a gun should feel just as natural in the hands of a German boy as a pen.'

The best boys were selected for training in one of the élite Adolf Hitler Schools for Party leadership, but at the age of 18 all of them went into Labour Corps for six months before embarking on the military training which was considered so vital a part of the Nazi New Order.

Above: German mothers in a *Lebensborn* home in Bavaria. Unmarried mothers in these homes were pressed to forgo all rights to their children and leave their care to the S.S.

Right: An idealized portrait of a member of the Hitler Youth.

Below: Members of the Hitler Youth line up for inspection.

Women in Nazi Germany

The Nazi Party, with its foundation of wartime comradeship and its militaristic activities, had little time for women, and they were not admitted as members. But far from letting women behave socially and develop culturally as they wished, the Nazis rigidly defined their role. It can be summed up briefly as *Kinde, Kirche, Küche* (children, church and kitchen), with the accent above all on children. 'German women wish in the main to be wives and mothers,' stated a widely-read summary of Nazi ideals. 'They do not wish to be comrades . . . They have no longing for the factory, no longing for Parliament, no longing for the office. A cosy home, a loved husband and a multitude of happy children are closer to their hearts.'

For many women this may be true, up to a point, but not when it is decreed by the State as the sole end in life. Besides, sinister motives lay behind this sentimental wording—the harsh fact of woman's total subordination to Adolf Hitler's militaristic and expansionist foreign policies. 'In my new Army,' he told a gathering of women, 'I have given you the finest fathers of children in the world.' For everything in life was to be subject to their biological role, to their procreational function as mothers of future German soldiers, and of females who would give birth to more soldiers. It was planned also that healthy childless German women over thirty should be ordered to submit themselves sexually to selected German men until they had borne at least four children. For all women, the Motherhood Cross was instituted: gold for eight children, silver for six and bronze for four.

This degradation of women to the level of breeding objects was accompanied by a puritan attitude to their appearance. Cosmetics, high heels, smart and colourful clothes, a *chic* turn-out roused Nazi anger. Smoking was taboo, and police warned women against it, while reminding them of their maternal functions. So short on sex appeal was the ideal Nazi woman, with her tightly braided hair, her scrubbed and shining face free of cosmetics, her rustic clothes and her dull mind, that sooner or later natural selection might well have intervened to defeat Hitler's aims and lower the birth rate.

Albert Speer, the realist technocrat, thought that women could work in the factories and raise arms production during the war, but Gauleiter Fritz Sauckel, Commissioner General for Labour, objected that their 'psychological and emotional life' and their child bearing capacity might be impaired. He pleaded this orthodox Nazi view to Hitler, who agreed with him. So urgently needed arms production fell, but the sacred function of German womanhood was believed to be unimpaired—at considerable cost to the efficiency of the Third Reich's War effort.

Left: Hitler sits surrounded by an eager crowd of youthful admirers in an obviously staged propaganda picture.

Above: Hitler greets a pretty German country girl. She typifies his ideal of the German wife and mother.

Nazism Breaks its Bonds

Officers and men of the German Army parade on
2 August 1934 for the swearing of the grim oath of
unconditional obedience to Hitler.

At about noon on 25 July 1934 a lorry loaded with uniformed men trundled into the courtyard of the Prime Minister's office, the Chancellery, in Vienna. The soldiers were S.S. members of the Austrian Nazi Party in uniforms procured from the Army. They were about to try to overthrow by force the right-wing Government of Chancellor Engelbert Dollfuss.

Invading the building, they cornered the unsuspecting Dollfuss, and one of them, Otto Planetta, shot him down. Dollfuss was then held incommunicado without priest or doctor until he died three hours later. His Cabinet ministers escaped and the Nazi putsch failed, largely because the Austrian Stormtroopers failed to stage their promised revolt as an act of revenge against the S.S. for the S.A. massacre in Germany.

Hitler, who had raised no objections to an enterprise which he knew would come sooner or later, at once found himself the centre of a storm of international protest. Fresh from an orgy of Wagnerian music at the Bayreuth Festival, he hastened to disavow complicity, and with Mussolini massing his army on the Austrian frontier, turned desperately for aid to his Vice-Chancellor, von Papen. 'We are facing another Sarajevo,' he shouted hysterically, in an appeal to von Papen to go to Vienna as Minister.

Reflecting that 'it must now be clear to the outside world that the rule of law had vanished not only within Germany, but was also being attacked beyond her frontiers,' von Papen nevertheless accepted the appointment, and went to Vienna to work in his own way for an *Anschluss*, or union.

The Western Powers now considered how best they should work to maintain Austrian independence and hold Germany to her international obligations in the light of Hitler's obvious wish to swallow the country, but perhaps Hitler divined intuitively that in the end he would have his way. For, five months earlier, Sir John Simon, the British Foreign Secretary, in what appeared to be the birth of the policy of appeasing Nazi Germany, had told the Commons that Germany's claim to equality of armaments 'cannot and ought not to be resisted'.

Nothing short of armed intervention could have stopped German rearmament, for Hitler was totally committed to it, and every sphere of German life was geared to it in greater or lesser degree. Weapons for the Air Force, the Army and the Navy were flowing from the factories. In July 1934 Hjalmar Schacht, President of the Reichsbank, had become Minister of National Economy as well, and the fruits of unified control of finance and industry in the field of rearmament were quickly seen. But the Wehrmacht, as Hitler had renamed the armed forces, was then far from ready for the war that British and French armed intervention on Austria's behalf would have meant, so Hitler reaffirmed his wish for peace and made a public disavowal of the Austrian Nazis.

Thus it was that the bright image of the national saviour that Goebbels had fashioned for Hitler was already stained, first by the S.A. massacre and now by the brutal killing of Dollfus, when Hitler moved to secure the Presidency and consolidate his dictatorship. For Hindenburg, in his 87th year, was now dying.

At once, on 1 August 1934, with the President on his

death-bed, the Nazi Cabinet passed an Act under the Enabling Law merging the offices of President and Chancellor. That same day Hitler flew to Neudeck to try to see Hindenburg before his death, perhaps to obtain his agreement to his succession to the Presidency while remaining Chancellor.

The old man was lying on his iron camp-bed in his Spartan bedroom holding his Bible when Hitler was shown in by Hindenburg's son Oskar. Told that Hitler had come to discuss one or two matters with him, he 'opened his eyes with a start, looked at Hitler, then shut his eyes again and did not say another word'. Hitler's last interview with Hindenburg had been no less humiliating than his earlier ones.

Hindenburg died next day, 2 August 1934, and the Cabinet, under Hitler's direction, immediately authorized another law which decreed that Chancellor Hitler had assumed the Presidency. Thus, in what was in effect a coup, Hitler had proclaimed his own succession and had become Commander of Germany's armed forces. He assumed the title of Führer and Reich Chancellor, declaring with a show of humility that the title of President was too closely associated with the dead Hindenburg.

Once wrapped in the presidential cloak, Hitler's first move was to call for the German people's acceptance in another of his staged plebiscites, arranged for 19 August 1934. But also on 2 August, having reached agreement with General von Blomberg, officers and men of the armed services were forced to swear an oath of loyalty to Hitler personally, an oath of a kind unprecedented in the Army's history. Everyone swore: 'Before God I swear this sacred oath, that I will render unconditional obedience to the Führer of the German Reich and people, Adolf Hitler, the Supreme Commander of the Armed Forces, and as a brave soldier will at all times be ready to lay down my life in fulfilment of this oath.'

What was the import of this oath that Hitler enforced upon the entire body of the armed forces? It was of the greatest significance, and for this reason Hitler called it 'sacred'. The previous oath, administered to recruits only, asked merely for loyalty and obedience to the Constitution and the President, at a time when the Constitution was intact and the President abided by it. But Adolf Hitler had already destroyed the Constitution and had illegally assumed the functions of the Presidency. And now he had forced the armed forces to swear that if need be they would give their lives in carrying out his commands blindly and without question.

Thus the oath taken on 2 August 1934 by the armed forces reduced their position virtually to that of helots, military slaves without hope, for the best they could do now was to enforce the Führer's will—or die in doing it. Faust sold his soul to Mephistopheles for the delights of the flesh. Germany's officers and men sold their souls to Hitler for a uniform, a gun and the law of death.

One might argue that patriotism and a greater Germany

Men of Germany's vastly expanded army march nine abreast with fixed bayonets past the Führer's hotel in Nuremberg during the 1936 Rally.

founded upon the defeat of other nations were the foundation of the oath, but there is not even this threadbare justification, for it was an absolutely unqualified oath binding the armed forces to do Hitler's bidding for any purpose he chose, even if necessary the destruction of the German people themselves.

As for the generals and the admirals, the day of the oath was for them their great turning point. They could have stood in Hitler's path, and in doing so could once more have endowed the armed forces with moral status in the Reich; for their failure to do so they paid by becoming Hitler's creatures – and betrayed their own people. 'For this betrayal,' the American historian Eliot Wheaton remarks, 'the army, the nation and the world were to pay a price beyond all calculation.'

Hitler, however, knew very well what he was doing, for he and his henchmen now had at their disposal an armed force subjugated to Hitler's will to a degree no army had ever before been bound to a leader in the history of the civilized world. And these armed forces, with a nod of assent from the British Government, were embarking upon a programme of rearmament that would make them a match for the combined military strength of the British Empire, Soviet Russia and the U.S.A.

On 19 August 1934, the German electorate were asked to approve by plebiscite the Act merging the offices of President and Chancellor. Of some 45 million voters, surfacing for air after a tidal wave of propaganda, over 38 million voted Yes. By no means as conclusive a vote as Hitler would have wished, it nevertheless enabled him to tell the world that the great majority of Germans agreed with the Act.

Meanwhile, the former trade unions, dissolved with the aid of the Stormtroopers in May 1933, had been replaced by the German Labour Front under Robert Ley. Encompassing employers and employees, capital as well as labour, it constituted a branch of the Nazi Party, and one of its functions was to organize six months' obligatory labour service in camps throughout Germany where youths of all classes worked at hard outdoor manual labour and drilled with spades as substitutes for rifles.

The objects were twofold to overcome barriers between the social classes as a step towards unifying the German people; and physically to harden and strengthen German youth as a prelude to the universal military training upon which Hitler was determined.

Meanwhile came the victorious plebiscite in the Saar coal-mining region. Formerly a part of Prussia, the Saar was detached under the Treaty of Versailles, with 15 years' exploitation rights for France to compensate her for the German destruction of French coal mines. On 13 January 1935, under a plebiscite held to decide whether the territory should stay under the League of Nations administration, return to Germany or go to France, 477,000 Saarlanders voted for Germany, 46,000 for the League and a ludicrous 2,000 for France.

A humiliation for France, it was no less a resounding victory for Germany, rather than the Nazis, and shouts of

Above: Hitler and Goering in conversation in 1935 at Karinhall, Goering's luxurious country residence. As can be seen, Goering's taste in leisure wear was nothing if not exotic.

Opposite page: A cavalry parade, headed by a drummer, trot through the streets of Nuremberg during the 1935 Rally.

Young Germans of the Labour Service march from their camp to forestry work. Youths of all classes proceded from the Hitler Youth to six months' labouring.

joy echoed across the country at this territorial gain, which had restored the valuable coalfields to Germany. Hitler declared in a radio speech that Germany would make 'no further territorial claims upon France,' but the French Government was hardly reassured now that the coal, essential to the Nazi rearmament programme, was in Hitler's hands and the Wehrmacht was already being strengthened by the flow of new weapons.

Consequently, early in March 1935, as a precaution, France extended compulsory military service from 18 months to two years. Hitler, again showing his brilliant political flair, announced on the same day (16 March) as the French extension became law the introduction of military conscription throughout Germany and the expansion of the Wehrmacht to 36 divisions, or about 360,000 men, in open defiance of the League of Nations.

To try to calm protests and fears abroad, Hitler made a speech in May stressing Germany's need and desire for peace. He declared solemnly that she had no intention of annexing Austria, and would respect the demilitarization of the Rhineland and the territorial clauses of the Treaty of Versailles. 'Whoever lights the torch of war in Europe

Goering and Streicher engage in an angry public quarrel at Nuremberg during the 1937 Rally. Hitler did nothing to prevent the rivalry and squabbling which were endemic among the Nazi hierarchy.

Police with rifles and fixed bayonets goosestep with military precision past a saluting Hitler after the Nuremberg Rally on 10 September 1937.

can wish for nothing but chaos,' he concluded in this deliberately deceptive speech.

One of the results of this speech was the Anglo-German Naval Agreement limiting Germany's surface fleet to 35 per cent and her submarine fleet to 60 per cent of the Royal Navy's—possibly worth while for Britain, but condemned in France and Italy, where it was seen as implied recognition of German naval rearmament and a breach of the Treaty of Versailles.

The Nazis were to exploit in the boldest and most brilliant way the disunity thus created, but first, in the late summer of 1935, other events which are today closely identified with the era came to a head. At the Nuremberg Rally of 15 September 1935 Hitler read out three new laws to the assembled multitude of specially summoned Reichstag deputies, Stormtroopers, S.S. and Party leaders.

The first law abolished the old Imperial flag and laid down that the swastika was now the official emblem of the Reich. The second, the Citizenship Law, established special conditions for German citizenship that deprived Jews of it. The third, a Law for the Protection of German Blood and German Honour, prohibited marriage and extramarital sexual intercourse between Germans and Jews and forbade the employment by Jews of German domestic servants below the age of 45. Significantly Hitler said that the

second of these two laws 'is an attempt to regulate by law a problem which, should the attempt fail, must then be handed over by law to the National Socialist Party for a final solution'.

These measures became notorious as the Nuremberg Laws. In passing them the Nazis had given formal legal assent to anti-Semitism, depriving German Jews of their citizenship and civil rights and thus robbing them of all protection that the State normally extended to its citizens. The Jews would henceforward be exposed without the slightest chance of redress to whatever fate was decreed for them.

The 1935 Nuremberg Rally ended with a menacing display by Germany's armed forces, in which some 100,000 men with armoured fighting vehicles, mechanized artillery, anti-aircraft guns and more than 100 bombers and fighter aeroplanes took part.

Throughout the winter of 1935–36 the Nazis were planning another coup, but this time they were to use armed force. In March 1936 came the propitious moment. The League of Nations had lost all authority owing to its failure to halt aggression in Abyssinia and Manchuria and to contain German rearmament. Hitler grew certain that fear of war and disunity among his opponents would enable him to reoccupy the Rhineland—demilitarized under the Treaty of Versailles—without a shot being fired. And once the Franco-Soviet Pact was ratified in late February he had the excuse of defensive action that he needed.

On 7 March 1936, at dawn, German units entered the Rhineland. France manned her defensive Maginot Line, then did nothing. Britain, whose squadrons of R.A.F. bombers could have hammered the Germans, also stayed her hand. The French city of Strasbourg was now within reach of German artillery.

That same day, while German guns rattled over the cobbled roads of the Rhineland, Hitler told the Reichstag deputies that he was proposing a 25-year non-aggression pact between Germany, France and Belgium, with Britain and Italy as the guarantor Powers. Once again he was throwing sand in the eyes of European statesmen: 'After three years I believe that today I can look upon the struggle for the restoration of German equality of rights as now concluded,' he told the Reichstag. 'In Europe we have no territorial claims to put forward.'

He then dissolved the Reichstag and called upon Germany to approve his policy in new elections of Nazi

German cavalry ride into the Rhineland in March 1936.

deputies. On 29 March 1936, out of 45·4 million voters, 44·4 million voted affirmatively. War or no war, the German people seemed solidly behind the Nazis.

Nazi Germany had emerged overnight as a power to be feared in Europe, for though France was militarily stronger her failure to hit back in defence of her interests was alarming for Poland, Austria and all of south-eastern Europe. For the Nazis it was one of the fruits of victory. Plans for aggression in Europe now preoccupied Hitler. While new weapons streamed off the factory assembly lines, expansion of the army was speeded up with the lengthening of compulsory military service to two years; and in October 1936 a Four Year Plan was inaugurated to achieve economic self-sufficiency in war.

Already the Nazis had achieved a brilliant economic recovery. Unemployment, which stood at six million when Hitler became Chancellor in January 1933, fell to 2·6 million by December 1934, then to 502,000 in October 1937 and was virtually non-existent at 164,000 in October 1938. The total number in employment during this period rose from 14·45 million in 1933 to 20·83 million in 1938.

This was achieved primarily by the credit manipulations of Dr Hjalmar Schacht, Reichsbank President and Minister of Economics, and a vast programme of public works which included Europe's first network of motorways, extensive land reclamation, afforestation and many huge new public buildings throughout the Reich, the biggest of which sprang up around Nuremberg. Added to this was the re-armament programme, with its chain of military airfields, its thousands of aircraft, tanks, guns and endless dumps of munitions.

Germany's workers, however, were not enabled to enjoy a higher standard of living, although there were, as we shall see, other compensations. Wages and prices were rigorously controlled, as indeed were imports and exports, so as to garner foreign currency for the purchase of vital raw materials. The takeover of Austria and Czechoslovakia was to provide an important dividend, and their substantial reserves of gold and foreign currency were immediately transferred to the Reichsbank.

Among Schacht's schemes for economic recovery were a system of values for the mark according to use, so that, for example, tourists and overseas buyers of German goods received a higher rate than the official rate of exchange;

Lord Halifax visits Goering in November 1937, shortly before he became British Foreign Secretary.

an extensive system of barter trading favourable to Germany in eastern Europe, which provided her with raw materials in exchange for manufactured goods; and the strictest control over the use of capital.

The second Four Year Plan, that of October 1936 headed by Goering, was designed to make Germany self-sufficient in time of war by the production of ersatz or substitute goods like the famous acorn coffee on a vast scale. It was only partially successful.

Provided he did not challenge the Nazi philosophy, life for the German worker was by no means grim or gloomy. 'We have become a poor people,' Goebbels declared in 1933, 'but nobody can deprive us of the joyful will to live, of the courage for work, of the intrepid optimism that overcomes obstacles.' And this summed up the day-to-day spirit of determination that inspired Germany in the thirties.

Nevertheless there were material compensations, mainly those of the Labour Front's Strength Through Joy movement, which existed to look after almost every moment of the people's leisure time, for private life in Nazi Germany was not encouraged. Strength Through Joy made available courses in a wide variety of subjects, including drama, the arts, sport, gymnastics, hunting and fishing and, in the summer, holiday cruises in the Mediterranean and the Baltic in one of the organization's own ships at prices the lowest-paid worker could afford. Low prices were achieved through mass participation and from a tax of 1·5 per cent on wages and salaries which went towards subsidies.

Having rebuilt Germany's economic status in Europe, the Nazis tried to extend her political influence. When the Spanish Civil War broke out on 17 July 1936, both Hitler and Mussolini sent military aid to General Franco, mainly in the form of aircraft. Mussolini at this time had completed his victorious campaign in Abyssinia, but at the cost of sanctions and other forms of hostility on the part of the Western Powers.

Hitler now exploited Mussolini's sense of isolation in Europe, first by recognizing his new Italian Empire in Abyssinia and then negotiating the Rome-Berlin Axis. He followed it in November with the Anti-Comintern Pact with Japan, the basis of a military alliance of the aggressor nations, which Italy would soon join. Meanwhile, Germany was building a wall of fortifications, the Siegfried Line, along her frontier with France in the Rhineland. Britain and France remained passive, their Governments having decided that Germany was protecting the West against Soviet Communism.

These fortifications weakened the security of all Europe east of the Reich, especially of Austria, which the Nazis had never stopped trying to subvert with money and violence. Relaxation of the tension between the Austrian and German Governments was promised in July 1936, when they signed a pact whereby Germany agreed not to intervene in Austrian affairs or to support the Nazis there. But this was another of Hitler's smoke screens, for at the same time Austrian Nazis were secretly being given support, and General von Fritsch was drafting plans for a projected invasion.

Hitler now moved to strengthen his control over the Wehrmacht. On 4 February 1938 he enforced the resignation of Generals von Blomberg and von Fritsch. He himself became combined Supreme Commander of the Armed Forces and War Minister; General von Brauchitsch became C.-in-C., and the subservient General Keitel was appointed Chief of Staff in place of von Fritsch. General Goering was promoted to Field-Marshal. Hitler thus ended the Army's traditional status of independence of the Government of the day and made it totally subservient to the Nazi State.

Eight days later he summoned Chancellor Kurt von Schussnigg of Austria to Berchtesgaden and bullied him with the threat of invasion to agree to including Nazi leaders in the Austrian Cabinet, a general amnesty for all Austrian Nazis in prison and the inclusion of the Austrian Nazi Party in the Government-sponsored Fatherland Front. Warning Schussnigg of Austria's helplessness, Hitler had told him: 'England will not lift a finger for Austria . . . And France? Well, two years ago when we marched into the Rhineland with a handful of battalions–at that time I risked everything. If France had stopped us then, we should have been forced to retreat . . . But now it is too late for France!'

Having been forced virtually to surrender Austria's independence, Schussnigg now saw a plebiscite as his last chance. He announced it on 9 March 1938 to enable the people, on Sunday, 13 March, to declare for a free and independent Austria. The news sent Hitler into one of his frenzied rages. If the Austrians declared for independence it would be a grave setback to his *Anschluss* plans. He determined to invade at once.

Having secured Mussolini's neutrality, he gave the orders which sent tanks, troop carriers and mobile guns clattering towards the Austrian frontier in the early hours of 11 March. That morning, in response to a message from Goering, Schnussnigg agreed to postpone the plebiscite, only to receive within half an hour an ultimatum that he must resign at once in favour of the Austrian Nazi Dr Arthur Seyss-Inquart, who had to be nominated within two hours–or the invasion would follow.

Schussnigg agreed, to save the catastrophe of war, but Austria's aged President Miklas refused to appoint Seyss-Inquart as Chancellor and no one else could be found to stand. Austrian Nazis swarmed threateningly into the streets; Goering sent angry messages; throughout the country a state of civil war neared, but not until midnight did Miklas finally agree to appoint Seyss-Inquart.

The invasion followed just the same. At dawn on 12 March 1938 German tanks and guns crossed the frontier, having been delayed by a series of breakdowns which left them helpless on the roadside. Hitler reached his boyhood town of Linz in the afternoon and spoke sentimentally of having fulfilled his mission of restoring his homeland to the Reich. Austria was annexed to Germany. There were cheers and flowers and tears of joy; then came Himmler, the S.S. and the Gestapo.

Led by Streicher, the Nazi 'old fighters' emerge through the smoke of the memorial urns at the Munich Feldherrenhalle during the annual homage to the Nazis who died in the abortive 1923 putsch.

Mass arrests followed; monarchists, Communists, priests, Jews, Freemasons, even Boy Scouts, were herded into the special trains that began running from Vienna, where more than 70,000 people were taken to Dachau. Among the prisoners were 165 former Austrian Government officials.

Himmler set up a concentration camp near the pretty village of Mauthausen on the north bank of the Danube, and by the end of the year it was ready for its first prisoners. Mauthausen was one of the most savage of all Himmler's camps for cruelty, torture and starvation. More than 30,000 people died there and in labour camps associated with it. Kurt von Schussnigg was punished by seven years' imprisonment in various concentration camps for having attempted as Chancellor to stand up to Hitler.

After Austria, the Nazis turned to Czechoslovakia and on 30 May 1938, at a secret meeting of a few chosen generals of the High Command, Hitler made his plans clear in a forthright speech. 'It is my unalterable decision to smash Czechoslovakia by military action in the near future,' he declared. 'From a military as well as a political standpoint the most favourable course is a lightning swift action as the result of an incident through which Germany is provoked in an unbearable way, for which at least part of world opinion will grant the moral justification of military action . . .' He added that the appropriate agencies must take action without delay to create a situation favourable to military action.

Italian support for this next move was arranged during Hitler's May 1938 visit to Rome, and Goebbels launched an intensive propaganda campaign on behalf of the German minority in Czechoslovakia, three million Sudetens, so called after the frontier region in which they resided. At the same time Konrad Henlein's Sudeten Nazi Party, financed from Berlin, was ordered to make demands that the Czech President Dr Benes would find impossible to accept.

Soon Hitler was making threats of military action and secretly he told his generals that his intention was to crush Czechoslovakia militarily during 1938. He used the September Nuremberg Rally – the 'Party Day of Greater Germany' – to whip up public feeling to a feverish degree and, in an interview with *Daily Mail* correspondent Ward Price on 17 September, he declared truculently: 'This Czech trouble has got to be ended once and for all, and ended now. It is a tumour which is poisoning the whole European organism. If it were allowed to go on, it would continue to infect international relations until they broke down in fatal collapse.'

The Wehrmacht began preparations, but the generals feared that Germany was not yet ready for the full-scale war against France, England and possibly Soviet Russia that this could involve. General Beck emerged as the leading conspirator in a plot to arrest the Führer, not on moral grounds but on those of expediency. When plans for the

Opposite, top: German troops enter Salzburg on 11 March 1938 to an apparently enthusiastic welcome.

Opposite, bottom: The grim aftermath of *Anschluss:* Jews are forced to scrub the streets in Vienna while grinning Nazis look on.

invasion went ahead, Beck demanded from Hitler a guarantee that no more military adventures would be undertaken. Hitler reminded Beck of the Army's oath of unquestioning obedience. Beck therefore resigned from his post of Chief of General Staff and forced Hitler to dismiss him by staying away from the War Ministry.

The Army generals, according to General Halder and to other accounts, now plotted to arrest Hitler in the War Ministry at the very moment when he gave the order for the Czech invasion. The other Nazi leaders were also to be held under arrest and a provisional military administration formed. Everything was apparently in readiness.

But now the British Prime Minister, Neville Chamber-

Kurt von Schussnig, Chancellor of Austria, who in February 1938 at Berchtesgaden was blackmailed by Hitler into taking Austrian Nazis into his Government.

lain, inadvertently torpedoed this conspiracy and saved Hitler. He proposed a meeting in Germany with Hitler to settle the issue by negotiation, in the mistaken belief that if Hitler could be appeased and war averted by sacrificing Czechoslovakia it must be done. The generals, led by the new Chief of Staff, General Franz Halder, therefore decided to wait, for, they told themselves, they would not be justified in acting if the Army was merely to march into territory already obtained through negotiation.

The course of the negotiations was dramatic. Briefly, at Berchtesgaden on 15 September Hitler agreed that arrangements could be worked out for the peaceful cession of the Sudetenland, but at the next meeting, at Godesberg on 15 September, where in June 1934 he had decided to launch the Röhm purge, Hitler changed his mind. He delivered an ultimatum to the effect that the Czechs must withdraw by 28 September from the Sudetenland or German forces would invade by 1 October. 'This is the last territorial demand I have to make in Europe,' Hitler told Chamberlain as the two men parted.

France, but not Britain, was bound by treaty to attack Germany if she made war on Czechoslovakia, but Britain promised to support France – if she fulfilled her obligations, which seemed doubtful. Soviet Russia and Poland were also ready to stand by France. Czechoslovakia had by now

Tanks and infantry stage a realistic mock battle to
demonstrate Panzer *Blitzkrieg* tactics at the
Nuremberg Rally of September 1938.

mobilized 1¼ million men. By 27 September the French Army was already half mobilized and the next day the British Admiralty ordered mobilization of the Fleet.

A clash seemed inevitable, but now several considerations persuaded Hitler to stay his hand. He saw Berlin crowds watch in silence the passage of one of his motorized units through the streets. It was a warning that war would not be popular. Admiral Raeder cautioned him on 27 September about the dangers of a major conflict, with Germany's forces at so great a numerical disadvantage compared with those of her possible adversaries. The next day brought a message from Mussolini requesting him to postpone action while examining new Anglo-French proposals for another 24 hours; and the British Ambassador then told Hitler that Britain would support France. Hitler finally agreed to put off military action for 24 hours.

The outcome was the notorious Munich Agreement of 29 September 1938, attended by Chamberlain, French Prime Minister Edouard Daladier, Hitler and Mussolini. The Czechs were not invited. Hitler gained most of his

Opposite page: Hitler addresses a force of 120,000
Stormtroopers at Nuremberg on 11 September 1938.
In his speech he made his first public reference to the
Sudeten Germans, pretext for the invasion of
Czechoslovakia.

demands; German forces marched into the Sudetenland on 1 October 1938 and took over the formidable Czechoslovak fortifications. About 11,000 square miles of Czech territory, in which there were 800,000 Czechs, was thus lost to Nazi Germany. For what it was worth, an Anglo-German declaration repudiating war was signed on 30 September.

The Nazi leaders now set about seizing the remainder of Czechoslovakia. Exploiting the racial differences between Slovaks, Czechs and the remaining Germans, the Nazi Press, orchestrated by Josef Goebbels, launched a campaign of lying reports of a Czech reign of terror and the 'bloody persecution of Germans'.

Hitler brusquely summoned the aged successor to Benes, Dr Emil Hacha, to Berlin, and at one o'clock in the morning of 15 March 1939 informed him in the presence of General Keitel that the German Army had been ordered to invade Czechoslovakia in five hours' time, at 6 a.m. Goering and Ribbentrop then took over the blackmailing of Hacha with the threat that unless the Czechoslovak Army withdrew and allowed German forces to enter the country in peace, the ancient city of Prague would be destroyed by bombing.

Hacha fainted. Hitler's quack physician, Dr Theo Morell, brought him round with a prompt injection. Hacha telephoned Prague and arranged with the Government that the Army should not resist the advancing Nazis. He then signed an abject communiqué stating that he

confidently placed the fate of the Czech people in the hands of the Führer'.

Two hours later, at 6 a.m., advance German mechanized units crossed the frontier and raced towards Prague, where Hitler arrived later in the day. That night Hitler slept in Hradschin Castle, palace of the old Bohemian kings, while the swastika hung over its ancient rooftops. The next day, proclaiming the German Protectorates of the provinces of Bohemia and Moravia, he declared that the Czechoslovak State had 'proved its inability to live its own internal life and in consequence has now fallen into dissolution'.

Hitler repudiated international protests at this brutal seizure of a genuinely peace-loving country with the lie that he had merely responded to the request of President Hacha. Slovakia now wisely bowed to the inevitable and on 16 March asked Hitler to take it under German 'protection'. Ruthenia, the remaining province, in which the Nazis had no interest, the Hungarians were authorized to occupy, while Poland hastily occupied the region of Tescha,

Above: Hitler's mountain retreat at Berchtesgaden, where he first presented his demands over Czechoslovakia to Chamberlain.

Opposite, top: The fateful meeting at Munich, 29 September 1938. From the left, Goering, Chamberlain, Mussolini, an interpreter, Hitler and Daladier, the French Prime Minister.

Opposite, bottom: S.S. troops jog trot at the end of a ten-mile training march in September 1938. A very important place was given to sport and physical fitness in the philosophy of the S.S.

Top: German troops are given a hostile reception in
Prague in March 1939.

Bottom: President Hacha of Czechoslovakia, an unwilling
guest of the triumphant Hitler, attends a march-past of
the German army in Prague in April 1939.

Opposite page: Hitler presents the standards at the last
Nuremberg Rally in 1939.

on her southern frontier. Thus the dismemberment of Czechoslovakia was completed.

As if this was not enough, world opinion in November was focused on the evil of Nazism in an especially shocking way. On the night of 9–10 November, Goebbels, in revenge for the murder of a Nazi diplomat by a young Jew in Paris two days earlier, gave orders for nationwide anti-Jewish riots, in effect a medieval pogrom. The Stormtroopers, held in check for so long, joyfully let themselves go once again. Hardly a synagogue was left standing, hundreds of Jewish business premises were looted and seized, over 30 Jews were murdered and many more were wounded. In what was named *Reichskristallnacht*, known as 'Crystal Night' on account of the hundreds of thousands of windows smashed, a large sum accrued to the Nazi treasury through official looting.

Meanwhile Hitler had begun to turn his attentions to Poland. Before the Nazis had completed their seizure of Czechoslovakia, Germany was persistently demanding from Poland the return of the free city of Danzig and the grant of special rights for a railway across the Polish Corridor, thus linking Germany with East Prussia.

At Berchtesgaden in January 1939 Colonel Jozef Beck, the Polish Foreign Minister, politely but very firmly assured Hitler that both of these demands were unacceptable, if only because the Polish people would never agree to them. Hitler promised that he would not proceed in Danzig with a *fait accompli* or create problems for the Polish Government. All was sweetness so far, instead of the usual threats of military action. Hitler was not ready for the latter until, on 15 March, he had overrun Czechoslovakia.

Then, on 21 March 1939, a new tone entered the talks. Ribbentrop, Germany's Foreign Minister, told the Polish Ambassador in Berlin that the issues between the two countries must be settled without delay. Poland still refused to give way, despite Germany's direct threats. Suddenly, on 31 March, Hitler received a shock which contradicted all his expectations. The British Government publicly promised Poland 'all support in their power' if its forces resisted action which threatened Polish independence–an assurance in which France joined.

Hitler was infuriated, but not stopped. On 3 April he secretly ordered General Keitel, Chief of Staff, to have plans for war against Poland ready by 11 September 1939, and to prepare for the defence of Germany's frontiers and for the seizure of Danzig. Then, on 28 April, in a Reichstag speech justifying his foreign policy, he accused Britain of seeing war with Germany as inevitable. He therefore

Far left: Ribbentrop and Stalin at the signing of the Nazi–Soviet non-aggression pact on 23 August 1939.

Left: On 1 September 1939 Hitler declared war on Poland. He told the Reichstag, 'I am now nothing but Germany's first soldier and I will not take off my uniform until victory is ours.'

denounced the 1935 Anglo-German Naval Agreement, a gesture which coincided with the launching of the great battleship *Tirpitz*. And since, he declared, Poland had refused to accept Germany's reasonable claims, he also tore up the German-Polish Pact of 1934.

A few days later, speaking as Supreme Commander and Minister for War, Hitler told the Wehrmacht chiefs in secret session that he was determined to attack Poland even if it did mean war with Britain and France. Plans for the attack on Poland were ordered to be brought forward to 20 August 1939.

The generals were alarmed, even though the Wehrmacht was far stronger than a year ago, for there was the danger of war not only with Britain and France, but also with Russia. Hitler, however, secretly held the trump card. On 22 August 1939 the Nazi-Soviet Non-Aggression Pact was announced and their fears were partially calmed. For Britain, and for France, who had also been negotiating at a snail's pace with Stalin, this reversal of Nazi anti-Communist policy was the biggest shock imaginable. 'The sinister news broke upon the world like an explosion,' Winston Churchill declared. 'It is a question whether Hitler or Stalin loathed it most . . . The antagonisms between the two systems were mortal.'

On 25 August 1939 Britain confirmed in a formal treaty with Poland the guarantees she had already given. In the hope that he could find some way of tempting the British to escape from their obligations, Hitler postponed the invasion of Poland until 1 September 1939. But at last Britain was determined on war.

Nazi Germany attacked Poland at dawn on 1 September 1939 and in a campaign lasting only a month demonstrated her new technique of *Blitzkrieg*, or 'lightning war' with tanks, infantry and aircraft–dive-bombers, bombers and fighters–in close support. Since this is not a book about the war, the sequence of the various campaigns in Europe will only be noted briefly, to be followed by a detailed look at the Nazis under the stress of war.

Britain and France declared war on 3 September 1939. In a broadcast the next day, transmitted to Germany, Mr Chamberlain said: 'In this war we are not fighting against you, the German people, for whom we have no bitter feeling, but against a tyrannous and forsworn régime which has betrayed not only its own people but the whole of Western civilization and all that you and we hold dear.' It was a fitting though belated declaration.

On 17 September Soviet forces surged into Poland to occupy the country's eastern regions allocated to them under the Pact. The Nazi generals held back their attack on France during the winter, deliberately delaying until the spring Hitler's wish for an offensive in the West. Then on 8 April 1940 they invaded Denmark and Norway, both to secure naval bases from which to operate against Britain, and to protect the transport of Swedish iron ore by sea down the Norwegian coast, upon which they depended for the war machine. Denmark fell at once. In Norway, where the British too had landed, six weeks sufficed to bring the Germans victory.

139

Above: In June 1940 after the fall of France, Hitler goes sightseeing in Paris. He told Speer, who accompanied him: 'It was the dream of my life to be permitted to see Paris.'

Opposite, top: German troops parade through occupied Warsaw in June 1940.

Opposite, bottom: Hitler cannot restrain his delight before the signing of the French armistice on 22 June 1940.

A pause of a few days followed the end of this campaign. Then began the Nazi *Blitzkrieg* on Holland, Belgium and Luxembourg. At half-past five in the morning of 10 May 1940 bombs rained down on both military targets and on cities and towns. Parachutists, infantry and tanks followed and five days later, by 15 May, resistance in Holland was over. On 27 May, after a brave resistance, the Belgian Army surrendered.

Meanwhile, on 14 May 1940, Germany had switched its main attack to France. The catastrophe that followed this next wave of *Blitzkrieg* is widely known. Allied forces fought à rearguard action back to Dunkirk, whence by 3 June 335,000 of them were evacuated across the Channel to Britain. Paris, not defended by French forces, was occupied on 14 June 1940 and on 22 June Marshal Pétain signed an armistice in the Forest of Compiègne in the same place and in the same railway coach in which the Germans had signed an armistice on 11 November 1918.

It was a savage irony, stage-managed by Hitler, that he could not resist. Four weeks later, master of Europe and perhaps thinking of Napoleon, he rewarded no less than 12 of his generals by promoting them to Field-Marshal.

They were von Beck, von Brauchitsch, Keitel, von Kluge, von Leeb, List, von Reichenau, von Rundstedt, von Witzleben and the Generals of the Luftwaffe Kesselring, Milch and Sperrle.

At the same time the High Command drew up plans for the invasion of Britain, called Operation Sealion, but the R.A.F.'s successful defeat of the Luftwaffe in the Battle of Britain caused Hitler to set aside this ambition and instead plan the immense undertaking of an attack upon Russia in 1941. Meantime the Nazis organized occupied Europe for Germany's economic, financial and military needs.

They clamped down on northern and western France, but the remainder under the armistice terms was left unoccupied, to be ruled by Marshal Pétain's pro-Hitler authoritarian régime at Vichy. Poland, Germany's bitterest enemy, the Nazis determined to rub off the map of Europe. The industrially valuable province of Silesia and the entire north-western half of Poland Hitler ordered to be incorporated into the Reich. The remainder, including Warsaw, he formed into a German colony called the General Government. The nation and all its resources were to become sources of slave labour and production for Nazi Germany.

Norway, Denmark, Holland, Belgium and Luxembourg, either subject to outright military government or ruled by puppet régimes backed by Nazi bayonets, were also to be ruthlessly exploited, though not with the same degree of savagery as Poland.

Himmler, the Gestapo and the S.S. now spread their tentacles throughout occupied Europe to install the grim rule of terror upon which the Nazi New Order depended.

THE RESISTANCE
Communists Church and Army

Left: Martin Bormann urges a shaken Hitler to take drastic action against suspects after the assassination attempt on 20 July 1944.

Only a few resolute individuals of great moral and physical courage opposed the Nazis. They risked not merely death, but death after prolonged torture at the hands of the Gestapo. The chief resistance bodies were the Conservative Nationalist military group, the Social Democratic and the Communist organizations, including the *Rote Kapelle* (Red Chapel), the Kreisau Circle and the individual leaders of the various anti-Nazi religious denominations.

Apart from hatred of Hitler and the Nazis there was little in common between them in terms of method and aims, but with the exception of the Communists their basic inspiration was Christian or humanist. The only real threat to Nazism was posed by the military group, which planned to assassinate Hitler. It included Colonel-General Ludwig von Beck, Army Chief of Staff until 1938; Admiral Wilhelm Canaris, chief of military intelligence, and his deputy, General Hans Oster; General Georg Thomas, Colonel Graf Claus von Stauffenberg, and Carl Goedeler, an outstanding political thinker.

These men saw Germany's future after the overthrow of Hitler as part of a European federation in which a probably authoritarian Germany would retain its new enlarged frontiers. They were linked with the non-militant Kreisau Circle—which concentrated on planning the government of the liberal Germany they hoped would arise after Hitler's fall—through such brave opponents of the Nazis as Count Helmut von Moltke and his wife, Count Peter von Wartenburg and Eugen Garstenmaier.

Above: Dr Carl Goerdler faces trial at the People's Court. Goerdler had been chosen by the July conspirators as the provisional Chancellor. Sympathy for Goerdler can be seen on the faces of the public.

Right: Colonel Claus von Stauffenberg, one of the principal members of the plot to assassinate Hitler on 20 July 1944.

Above: Hitler shows Mussolini the damage caused by the unsuccessful assassination attempt of July 1944. Although shaken by the explosion, Hitler was able to greet Mussolini only a few hours after it took place.

The *Rote Kapelle* Communist opposition group worked alone to overthrow the Nazi régime and to replace it by a Soviet Germany dominated by Soviet Russia. Directed from Moscow through cells in France and Holland, it mainly spied for Russia and made no attempts to overthrow the Nazis through a coup. Its chief, Lieutenant Schulze-Boysen of the Luftwaffe, sent Moscow precise details of German aircraft production and airborne forces until he was caught by the Gestapo and hanged in December 1942. The *Rote Kapelle* was smashed, but Communist cells survived up to the end of Nazism, organizing industrial sabotage with the Gestapo always on their heels.

During 1943 the military group planned no less than six attempts on Hitler's life, all of which either failed or were postponed. Outstanding was Fabian von Schlabrendorff's smuggling of a bomb into Hitler's aircraft on 13 March 1943, which failed only through a faulty detonator. Colonel von Stauffenberg placed the bomb that failed to kill Hitler on 20 July 1944.

The Church never advocated rebellion against the Nazis, but tried firmly to defend Christianity, as when for example, Martin Niemöller publicly repudiated Hitler's claim that the German people were his responsibility, with the statement that nobody could take from the Church what God had given it. Stauffenberg expressed his dilemma with the words: 'Who ever dares to act must realize that he will probably go down to history as a traitor. Yet if he fails to act he will be a traitor to his own conscience.'

Death Works Overtime

Auschwitz concentration camp was opened on 14 June 1940. By 1945, 300,000 people had lost their lives there.

Heinrich Himmler had been steadily worming his way to power through the Nazi jungle while Hitler, despite the fears of many of his generals, was conquering Europe—Austria, Czechoslovakia, Poland, Norway, Denmark, Holland, Belgium, Luxembourg and France. On 20 April 1934 as *Reichsführer-S.S.* Himmler had won control of the entire political police and on 17 June 1936 he had added supreme command of all German police to his personal empire. War and extreme racialism—the *Herrenvolk-Untermenschen* obsession—and the extension of Himmler's responsibilities geographically and administratively, combined to inflate him to the status of a Nazi overlord second only to Hitler, now that Goering was eclipsed following his failure in the Battle of Britain.

People—all the millions of men, women and children who after mid-1940 came under the Nazi jackboot—were his raw material. Throughout the occupied territories, as well as in Germany, he decreed by means of S.S. and police terror the repression of dissidents; the organization, later with the aid of the Manpower Plenipotentiary Fritz Sauckel, of a workforce of slaves in factories and camps; the return of 'racial' Germans in occupied territories to the Reich; the colonization of occupied territories, and the final solution of the Jewish question by a policy of genocide.

Hitler's decree of 7 October 1939 for the Strengthening of Germandom laid down the aims of Nazi policy in occupied Poland. In it he ordered Himmler, as Reich Commissar for the Strengthening of Germandom, to establish new German settlements and to 'eliminate the injurious influence of nationally alien population groups constituting a danger to the Reich and for German society'.

The cruel reality behind this turned out to be the forcible removal of Polish and Jewish inhabitants from the occupied territory and its speedy colonization by German families. And behind this, again, lay the demands of the Nazi New Order in Europe, then in the process of organization on behalf of the *Herrenvolk*.

Hitlerian cultural and social implications apart, the New Order in short term involved the coordination throughout Europe of all economic and industrial resources to supply weapons, food and uniforms to the Wehrmacht for the coming onslaught against Soviet Russia. And Himmler devised a methodical plan for carrying out the order for 'Strengthening of Germandom'.

In November 1939 he appointed seven Reich Commissioners for the occupied Polish territory, mainly esteemed Nazis who had distinguished themselves as higher S.S. and police leaders. One of them, S.S. Lieutenant-General Erich von dem Bach-Zelewski, was entrusted with the Germanization of the province of Silesia in south-eastern Poland.

According to Himmler's order of 30 October 1938, his duties included the removal by February 1940 of all Jews and 'hostile elements among the Polish population', and the settlement of incoming Germans. Jews and Poles to be 'resettled' were authorized to take only hand baggage with them, excluding foreign currency, precious metals, jewellery, works of art, furniture, household linen, etc.

Von dem Bach-Zelewski coordinated his deportation plans with the notorious Adolf Eichmann in the Gestapo department which dealt with the 'security and political problems' arising out of the resettlement. Von dem Bach-

Zelewski worked quickly and by 4 January 1940 one of his officials was reporting to Eichmann that 125,000 Jews in the south-eastern region were being deported to the General Government area of Poland.

By the end of August, S.S. units had begun the removal of 20,000 Polish farmers and their families in one particular district of the south-eastern region whose farms, homes and property were to be occupied by Germans.

Convoys of lorries with S.S. men cordoned off peasant villages, smallholdings and farms, drove the inhabitants into lorries with blows from rifle butts, then, having looted the property, delivered the Poles to the railway station, whence they were transported to the General Government region and dumped. Punctilious to a degree, von dem Bach-Zelewski invariably welcomed the incoming Germans.

Himmler now began to try to implement his plan for a class of German warrior-farmers in Poland to act as a bulwark against 'Slav and Asiatic hordes' in the East. Special S.S. action commandos, the *Sonderkommandos*, began the mass murder of the Polish élite—landowning aristocrats, lawyers, doctors, priests, teachers, artists, military officers, businessmen—according to Hitler's order that 'whatever we can find in the shape of an upper class in Poland is to be liquidated'. The Polish upper classes, no less than Polish Jewry, were decimated.

At the same time the S.S. Special Action Groups turned their attention to the cities in western Poland. The 270,000 inhabitants of Poznan, for example, were forced to leave their homes and were transported to camps in the General Government area. Throughout Poland the Nazis suppressed political parties, and closed universities, libraries and art collections, either looting the contents or officially removing them to Germany. All schools, with the exception of a small number of primary schools, were closed down, and the German Criminal Code was imposed with death sentences for minor offences.

From the Baltic states, Soviet-occupied eastern Poland, the Austrian Tyrol and Yugoslavia, families of German descent were recalled to the Reich to colonize these new 'German' lands in Poland.

A swift expansion of the number of concentration camps naturally followed in occupied Europe. In Germany, up to September 1939, Himmler and Goering between them had established six main camps, with at that time some 30,000 prisoners, although at least twice as many had by then become victims of the camps, and subsequently had been released, had died or had been murdered.

The seizure of Austria and Czechoslovakia led to a sudden and sharp increase in camps and to a new total of 162,700 prisoners. Then it was Poland's turn. Camps were established at Belzek, Treblinka and Wolzek in the General Government area. Von dem Bach-Zelewski realized that the efficient administration—to use the then current euphemism—of the south-eastern region demanded a camp there also.

Fortunately, a Polish military barracks was available near the town of Oswiecim, about 175 miles south-west of Warsaw. With characteristic thoroughness Himmler sent to inspect the site officials of his Inspectorate for Concentration Camps, who submitted a thorough report on its suitability. The Camp was given the German name of Auschwitz and the first trainload of prisoners arrived there on 14 June 1940.

S.S.-Haupsturmführer Rudolf Höss, who was condemned to death at Nuremberg, was appointed Commandant. On 6 July 1940, according to a report on von dem Bach-Zelewski published by the *Polish Journalists' Cooperative*, a prisoner named Tadeusz Wiejowski escaped. Shamefacedly, Höss reported this seeming neglect of duty on his part when the overbearing von dem Bach-Zelewski visited the camp, explaining in mitigation the hostile attitude of the 'fanatically Polish' local people.

The sequel illustrates how arbitrary sentences became the norm in Polish territory occupied by the Nazis. At once, von dem Bach-Zelewski ordered the summary execution by shooting of five civilians suspected of aiding the prisoner's escape, and the immediate shooting of all men found in the wired-off camp foreground. Women and children found there were to be arrested, and the whole territory within a five-mile radius was to be 'cleaned of suspected rabble'. Von dem Bach-Zelewski emphasized that the executions should be 'carried out in such a way as to be a warning to all having similar intentions'.

But Rudolf Höss, then a nervous and apprehensive official, obtained the orders in writing and, still uncertain of his responsibility, asked the Inspectorate of Concentration Camps in Berlin on what date the executions should be carried out. The outcome was that the condemned were instead ordered to be first flogged and then sent to the concentration camp at Mauthausen for five years. A slow death was substituted for a quick one.

Men of the S.S. Death's Head Battalions, the *Totenkopfverbände*, were until 1934 given the task of guarding the camps, harassing the prisoners and administering the brutal and arbitrary sentences—flogging, torture and death—described by Himmler as 'fighting the subhumanity'. *S.S.-Oberführer* Theodore Eicke was until 1934 Commandant of Concentration Camps. Eicke trained his subordinates to hate the prisoners with unlimited ferocity as 'enemies of the State'.

Rudolf Höss, an ever-willing subordinate, learned the lesson well and Auschwitz became an especially notorious camp, if this was possible, in which, according to Gerald Reitlinger, the names of an estimated 363,000 people were registered on the books between February 1940 and January 1945. Of these 280,000 died, were murdered or killed themselves.

Prisoners in the camps were forced to flog other prisoners, and were punished themselves if they shirked doing so with all their strength. They were bribed with a cigarette or two to act as the hangmen of prisoners sentenced to death for some trivial offence. Work, carried out under the supervision of privileged prisoners named *Kapos*, and the S.S., included railroad construction, quarrying, road mending and later factory work. It lasted as much as 14 hours a day and had always to be performed at the double. Exhausted prisoners were usually shot.

A shaven-headed prisoner at the Sachsenhausen camp is carefully photographed on arrival.

Emaciated prisoners sprawl weakly on their tiered bunks at Dachau concentration camp.

The world heard about these horrors in the postwar years through the Nuremberg Trials and numerous books. The questions that arose and are still being asked were: who among the Germans, Nazis or not, were found to carry out tasks of constant inhumanity, involving torture and killing in cold blood day after day? And secondly, what place did the camps have in the Nazi scheme of things, the much-vaunted New Order?

The camps were nothing less than inevitable in the Nazi scheme of things in Germany and occupied Europe. Apart from the Germans who opposed Hitler throughout the Nazi era, all of whom it was felt needful to imprison or 're-educate', there were Jews, resistance people in Western Europe and finally the Poles, Ukrainians and all the Slav races in occupied Russia. In due course all of them became material either for labour camps or for the extermination camps, like Treblinka and Auschwitz after 1941.

To understand the compelling Nazi need for labour and extermination camps we must recall the *Herrenvolk* basis upon which the war against Russia was launched. Hitler, his Cabinet and the High Command began preparations for it in the summer of 1940 after the failure of the Battle of Britain and the postponement of Operation Sealion. Hitler issued an order making 15 May 1941 the final date for all preparations for *Fall Barbarossa*, code word for the lightning campaign to conquer the Soviet Union.

On 30 March 1941, Field-Marshal Keitel issued the operational orders for the campaign and declared: 'On the territory of operations the *Reichsführer-S.S.* receives, with Hitler's consent, special tasks resulting from the fight which will take place between the two systems.'

The 'special tasks' were the transportation to extermination camps or the immediate murder of the local population, including resistance groups, partisans, Jews and political commissars. For this purpose, in May, some four weeks before the invasion, special operational task forces of the *Sipo*, or S.S. Security Police, and the S.D., or S.S. Security Intelligence Section, called *Einsatzgruppen*, were formed and detailed to move into the U.S.S.R. immediately behind the Wehrmacht.

At the same time, Hitler signed a decree authorizing, at the discretion of *Sipo* officers, mass retaliatory executions of civilians, without trial or investigations, in the territories to be occupied. Himmler coolly informed the higher S.S. leaders who had been appointed to command these operations in the rear of the Army that by the time the campaign was over, the Slav race, as a result of their work, would number 30 million people less, and 'the biological danger threatening Germany would be removed'.

With the invasion of Soviet Russia on 22 June 1941 came the *Einsatzgruppen* (Special Action Groups), following in the rear of the *Panzer* and motorized infantry divisions. They were committed to programmes of mass extermination of men, women and children.

S.S.-Gruppenführer Franz Stahlecker, commanding *Einsatzgruppe A* on the Leningrad front, and in the Baltic countries, was responsible for killing 221,000 people in the first two years of the War, mainly by shooting. In the central sector, ruled by the former *Kriminalpolizei* Chief in the Reich, *S.S.-Gruppenführer* Arthur Nebe, commanding *Einsatzgruppe B*, with headquarters first at Minsk then at Smolensk, scores of thousands of the Russian population were also killed. But Nebe was a member of the anti-Hitler resistance and he sabotaged this mass slaughter whenever he could.

Captured political commissars and G.P.U. (Soviet Secret Police) were regarded as 'criminals' to be shot out of hand in the war the Nazis were waging to destroy 'Bolshevism'. The Army's regulations as to the treatment of civilians held good only in areas where Soviet and German units were actually locked in battle. As little as five or six miles to the rear in the operational areas Himmler's men were free to commit the most hideous crimes, to murder innocent villagers, townsfolk and prisoners of war. Paramount was the slaughter of Jews. No Jew anywhere in the invaded Soviet territories was to be left alive. In the Russian city of Kiev, for example, 33,700 Jews were gunned down in three months in September 1941.

Himmler attended a mass execution of Jews at Minsk in the summer of 1941. Seeing for the first time the all too terrible reality behind abstractions and euphemisms like

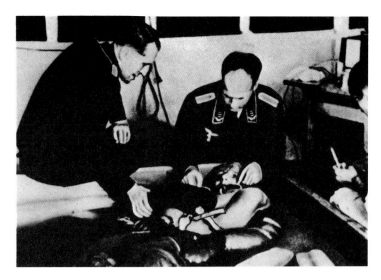

Above: One of the many appalling experiments carried out with Jewish guinea pigs by Dr Holz at Dachau. This is a 'freezing' experiment.

Right: A young Polish civilian calmly faces death as a Nazi executioner of the *Einsatzgruppen* shoots him on the edge of a mass grave. Mass executions emptied the countryside so that German settlers could move in.

'resettlement' and 'special treatment', Himmler – according to von dem Bach-Zelewski at Nuremberg – lost his self-control, grew hysterical, nearly fainted and appeared to be deeply shocked. But there was no question of an end to the killings. Himmler gave orders for the installation of gassing chambers at the extermination camps – Treblinka, Belzek, Auschwitz and elsewhere. Out of sight, in the grey concrete halls of death, the helpless inmates of the camps were killed in batches of up to 2,000 people at a time.

Rudolf Höss testified in a matter-of-fact way at Nuremberg that, having been ordered to instal 'extermination facilities' at Auschwitz in June 1941, he first visited Treblinka, also in Poland, to study the system and learned that 80,000 people had been gassed there in six months, mostly Jews from the Warsaw ghetto. 'He used monoxide gas and I do not think that this method was very efficient. So at Auschwitz I used Cyclon B, which was a crystallized prussic acid dropped into the death chamber ... After the bodies were removed, our special commandos took off the rings and extracted the gold from the teeth of the corpses.' The money thus obtained was credited to a secret S.S. account in the Reichsbank and helped to create a special treasury for Himmler's expanding empire.

In 46 days of the summer of 1944, some 6,500 Hungarian Jews alone were to lose their lives daily at Auschwitz, apart from those from other countries. While Hitler's dream of a 'racially pure' Europe and western Russia dominated by the *Herrenvolk* faded fast, his anti-Semitic rage drove *Einsatzgruppen* and S.S. to the very limits of their power to exterminate. Gerald Reitlinger's authoritative *The Final Solution* puts the numbers of those slaughtered in the death camp infernos at between 4·2 and 6·2 millions.

It was a mark of Himmler's diabolical efficiency that barely 3,000 men constituted these *Einsatzgruppen* and that the entire system of concentration camps was run by a mere 70,000 S.S. Who were the *Einsatzgruppen*? To begin

with they were volunteers from either the S.D. or the Gestapo; they also came from occupied Latvia and the Ukraine in search of good rations, safety from enemy bullets and artillery, or for the satisfaction of sadistic impulses and insatiable hatred for humanity.

Their officers included men of the professional classes – an alcoholic architect, an unemployed opera singer, an unfrocked parson and a number of strays from the academic world. The senior commanders were top Nazis, sometimes willing, sometimes forced to accept the appointment because they had incurred the hostility of someone like Himmler.

A number of them had been recruited from the Nazi euthanasia death camps where, in the first two years of the war, about 150,000 German citizens, whose only crime was to suffer from some kind of incurable mental illness, were murdered by euthanasia injections. This was a project upon which in the presumed interests of a virile and healthy nation Hitler had set his heart. Himmler therefore sent medical officers from the S.S. or Death's Head units to visit Germany's mental homes to choose victims who were sent to one of the six euthanasia centres. Vehement public and private protests, curiously enough, were effective, and when they came from both Protestant and Catholic Church leaders, influential people like Prince Philip of Hesse, an old friend of Himmler's from his days of innocence, this heinous practice was given up in August 1941.

In the fields of esoteric inquiry into Germany's past, Himmler was easily duped. These activities ranged from the *Ahnenerbe*, an S.S. institute for research into 'German ancestral heritage' including aspects of the mother cultus

Expansion of Hitler's Empire

▪ Original territory of Germany, January 1938.

▫ Original territory of the satellite and allied States, January 1938.

▪ Territory under German, Italian, and satellite occupation in the second half of 1942.

which dabbled in occultism, to astrology in all its ramifications, as well as telepathy and extrasensory perception. Once, Himmler heard about a German mother who had, it appeared, borne three children after the age of 48. To Himmler such devotion to the Reich and to German motherhood seemed worth extolling. He had the mother significantly rewarded and for the father, Sigmund Rascher, he found a safe place in the S.S.

In due course, as Rascher's talents emerged, he was promoted to Dachau, where he carried out tests on the resistance of living people to temperatures below freezing point; and Himmler was pleased with his conscientious protégé. But one day early in 1944 the truth came out. Rascher was no father, nor was Frau Rascher a mother. Himmler had been the victim of a cheap trick, for the children had in fact been procured from an orphanage. So wounded was Himmler that he had Rascher flung into an underground cell at Dachau. His ultimate fate was no better than that of any other transgressor in Nazi Germany.

On 25 August 1943, Himmler's appointment as Interior Minister of the sagging Third Reich, in succession to Wilhelm Frick, confirmed officially the immense power he had been exercising for the past several years. His only rival, now that Goering was a fading star, was the bear-like Martin Bormann, Party Secretary and Hitler's personal aide, who never left the Führer's side and more than anyone else was capable of influencing him. It was Bormann who, whenever possible, checkmated Himmler's moves to add still more to his seemingly impregnable position in the Reich and to strengthen the ramifications of what has been called the S.S. State—the State within a State—which was Himmler's special creation.

Its main features were the labour, concentration and extermination camps, the Gestapo, the S.S., the S.S. Security Police, and the S.S. Intelligence Service with its ubiquitous system of spies threaded into every section of national life, including the S.S. itself; and finally, the mass murder squads, the *Sonderkommandos* and the *Einsatzkommandos*. The special characteristic of the S.S. State, a byproduct of the struggle for its ideals, was death.

Himmler's S.S. empire at its zenith stretched from the Pyrenees through central Europe across Poland to Leningrad, the approaches to Moscow, and to Stalingrad and the Crimea in the south. Himmler travelled on inspection tours in a train unsmilingly labelled 'Heinrich'. He held sway over armies too, and by late 1942 had extended to eight divisions the *Waffen-S.S.*, whose divisions were armed on the same weapon scale as a German infantry division.

When it came to munitions, Himmler wanted to be free from dependence on the interfering generals, for obvious reasons. He therefore sought authority from Hitler in 1942 to use his concentration camp prisoners for munitions production, but fearing that this might grow into a menace to his own supremacy, Hitler at first refused.

Meanwhile Goebbels had come up with the proposal

that as an aid to higher war production, not only gypsies and Jews should be worked to death in production centres in the camps, but thousands of other prisoners as well. Albert Speer, Minister for War Production, proposed that Himmler should supply prisoners to work in munitions factories and that up to 8 per cent of production should be supplied to the *Waffen-S.S.* Without a tremor of his pince-nez, at a meeting on the issue, Himmler advanced his interests by proposing that anyone of any nationality in 'protective custody' and any German serving at least eight years' imprisonment should be placed in this category. The Reich Minister of Justice, Otto Thierack, raised no objections to this startling proposal. The agreement, essentially a very private one, which was never embodied in a written decree, was called 'The Delivery of A-Social Elements to the *Reichsführer-S.S.* to be Worked to Death'.

Himmler's higher S.S. and police leaders now had a terrible weapon with which to decimate the populations of the occupied eastern territories; anyone could now be classified as anti-social and be flung into Himmler's labour camps or the murderous régime of the factories. As a result, scores of thousands of Poles, Ukrainians, Russians, Balts and Jews were rounded up and sent to work almost round the clock making munitions on starvation rations. Thousands of them died every month of starvation, exhaustion and disease, or were executed.

Between June and November 1942 some 136,700 people were reduced to slavery in the camps or factories. By 30 November only 27,987 still lived, 70,610 having died from exhaustion, illness or starvation, 9,267 having been executed and 28,846 gassed. Seeing in this a threat to the flow of munitions for the *Waffen-S.S.*, Himmler ordered an investigation and the trial of the camp commandants who had broken the regulations, which of course they had always done, and with Himmler's knowledge. But now that this loss of valuable labour was inexpedient, Himmler ordered the shooting of some of them, including Erich Koch, commandant of Buchenwald, *pour encourager les autres*.

By early 1943, in any case, the fine fighting qualities of the *Waffen-S.S.* divisions, like *Das Reich* on the Russian front, had persuaded Hitler that with armour they would do even better. Ignoring the objections of the High Command, he authorized their equipment with tanks, armoured troop carriers and mobile artillery, all the weapons in fact of a *Panzer* division. Munitions and weapons also reached the *Waffen-S.S.* from the factories, under Himmler's agreement with Speer, so that he was able to expand it to about 500,000 men by May 1944, not long before the Allied landings in Normandy, though only about half of them were Germans from the Reich.

'Racial Germans'—Balts, Danes, Dutch, Croats and Hungarians—persuaded to volunteer by every kind of inducement, made up the rest of what Himmler was beginning to regard as his 'European army'. But defeat on the Russian front in 1943–44 and the huge casualties among the S.S. no less than the *Wehrmacht* divisions started to lose Himmler the loyalty of his *Waffen-S.S. Obergruppenführer*.

Hitler confers with Sepp Dietrich, commander of the *Leibstandarte-Adolf Hitler*, in the situation room at his military headquarters in East Prussia.

The long-awaited Allied D-Day landings were launched successfully in the early hours of 6 June 1944 along a 30-mile stretch of the coast of Normandy, and by 12 June the invaders had achieved a bridgehead ten miles inland along a front of 80 miles. The landing, the subsequent break-out and the heavy defeat of the German armies by the onrushing British and United States forces, as well as the defeats on the Russian front, brought to a head the long-standing hostility to Hitler of a number of generals and other senior officers.

There had been other opposition groups, but sooner or later the Gestapo had discovered and eliminated them. The Wehrmacht group had been intermittently active since Munich and included, apart from General von Beck, Colonel von Stauffenberg, General Oster and Admiral Canaris of the Abwehr (military intelligence); General Georg Thomas, General von Brauchitsch, Carl Goerdeler, the political thinker and former mayor of Leipzig, Field-Marshal von Witzleben, Ulrich von Hassell, former German Ambassador in Italy, and Julius Leber, a remarkable German Socialist much admired by Stauffenberg.

Count Klaus von Stauffenberg emerged in 1943 and,

Opposite, top: Jews are forced at gunpoint to leave the Warsaw Ghetto in 1943. They were deported to concentration camps.

Opposite, bottom: German troops set fire to the Warsaw Ghetto in May 1943 after an armed Jewish uprising.

together with General von Tresckow, he it was who inspired the 20 July 1944 bomb plot. According to it, after the Führer's assassination, Leber and von Beck were to form a provisional Government with the latter as regent, Leber, the Socialist, as Chancellor, and von Witzleben as C.-in-C., while power was seized in Berlin, Munich, Cologne and Vienna. Earlier attempts had either failed or been at the last moment postponed owing to changes in the Führer's plans.

Fabian von Schlabrendorff, another of the conspirators, had placed a bomb in Hitler's aircraft on 13 March 1943, but although the device was set and Hitler took off according to plan the bomb failed to explode owing to the unforeseen effects of change in air pressure through altitude upon the detonator.

Hitler had undergone a marked decline in health during the War and often predicted his early death, but there were no signs that sickness or disease would end his life in the immediate future. He worried unendingly about his heart, his stomach and his bowels, and was forever checking his pulse and dutifully taking the shoal of pills and medicines prescribed for him by his personal physician, Dr Theodore Morell.

Some of these pills, notably an anti-gas preparation containing strychnine, though beneficial in small quantities, became dangerous when taken continually in the substantial doses evidently prescribed by Morell. However, there can be no doubt that Hitler sustained himself at this time with the aid of Morell's drugs. So Hitler's ill-health worsened, either in spite of Morell's treatment

151

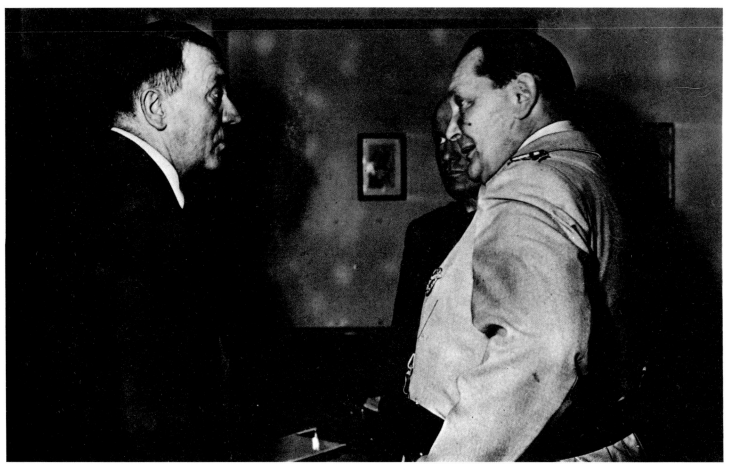
A shocked Hitler greets Goering and Mussolini, after the attempt on his life in July 1944.

or because of it. Spending his days and nights in 1943 and 1944 in the underground bunker of his East Prussian headquarters, Hitler also grew oversensitive to daylight, suffered intensely from headaches and sleeplessness, lost his zest, vitality and nervous energy, could not control a violent tremor in his left hand, and was mentally and physically exhausted.

This then was the ghost of the man who had recreated Germany according to his own dreams for it—the Führer, who was still Germany's Supreme Commander, directing the Wehrmacht in costly and ineffectual last-ditch battles against Soviet Russia and the Allies.

By early 1944, the conspirators, urged on by von Stauffenberg, had perfected their plans and now awaited their chance to try to save Germany, or themselves, depending on whether love for the Fatherland or self-love prompted them.

The opportunity to assassinate Hitler was eventually seen in an Army staff conference to be chaired by the Führer in the so-called *Wolfsschanze* military headquarters in one of the gloomy and oppressive forests which stretch across East Prussia. Whole books have been written about the attempt, although the detailed account given by Professor Sir John Wheeler-Bennett is outstanding.

Briefly, Klaus von Stauffenberg, conspicuous for the black patch over his eye and a hand missing through wounds sustained in North Africa, entered the guest house where the conference was due to be held—instead of in the underground room, then unavailable owing to alterations. He greeted Hitler and with extraordinary coolness placed the briefcase holding the bomb under the heavy wooden table, with the remark: 'I will leave this here for the moment; I have to make a telephone call.'

The timing device had been previously set and there were only two or three minutes to go. General Heusinger neared the end of the report he was reading and General Keitel looked around for Stauffenberg, whose turn it was to speak next. But he had not yet come back from telephoning, nor was he in the anteroom. Meanwhile, as doubt and then suspicion formed in Keitel's mind, Colonel Heinz Brandt, not a party to the plot, casually pushed von Stauffenberg's deadly briefcase further away from him—and thus from Hitler.

A second or two later at 12.40 p.m. came a tremendous explosion, apparently destroying the hut. Stauffenberg and his aide, Werner von Haeften, immediately drove to the airport to fly to Berlin. Another of the conspirators, General Erich Fellgiebel, should now have telephoned Berlin with the news that the operation had been successful and that Hitler was dead, so that the plotters could put their plans into action; but he failed to do so.

Fellgiebel unaccountably also failed to destroy the telephone communications centre at the headquarters, the most vital move after the bomb explosion. It would have meant that, whether or not Hitler lived, his entire entourage, including the Army High Command, were cut off and rendered powerless.

The news reached Berlin that the explosion had in fact occurred, and later, at about 3.30 p.m., came a telephone call from von Haeften to the effect that Hitler was dead. The *Valkyrie* operation to take over power went into partial effect. Then came the contradictory news from General

Field-Marshal Erwin von Witzleben, one of the July conspirators. During his trial his belt and braces were removed so that he was forced to hold up his trousers. He was put to death by hanging with a noose of piano wire from a meathook, on 8 August. The executions were filmed for Hitler to see that same evening.

Above: Hitler argues desperately with his generals in March 1945. The Soviet forces were now only 45 miles east of Berlin, but Hitler continued to marshal non-existent divisions on the maps in the bunker beneath the Chancellery.

Keitel that Hitler had survived the attempt. He had suffered slight burns, damaged eardrums and shock, but was not prevented from entertaining the fallen Mussolini, who had arrived early in the afternoon.

Fanfares of commands and countermands now flashed back and forth across Germany as both sides in the conflict sought to impose their will, but gradually the news that Hitler was indeed alive brought all the forces of the Reich to bear against the conspirators, gathered in the General Staff building in the Bendlerstrasse. General Fromm, who was implicated in the plot, tried to save his skin by forcing General Beck to kill himself and court-martialling and executing von Stauffenberg and two other conspirators by firing squad outside in the courtyard.

Himmler, who had himself been involved in tentative negotiations with the Allies to arrest Hitler and make peace, now for a short time saw Hitler's escape as a sign from Providence that he would yet save the Reich. In a frenzy of remorse he unleashed a reign of terror throughout Germany. Hitler personally ordered von Witzleben and several other generals and officers to be hanged by piano wire attached to meat hooks in a common death cell. Their death agonies were filmed and shown to Hitler, whose thirst for revenge was now insatiable.

General Fromm was beheaded, and as the net of revenge and suspicion was flung even wider, Hjalmar Schacht and the former Chief of Staff, General Halder, were arrested and flung into concentration camps. Himmler, whose gunmen had meanwhile carried out executions estimated at several hundred, emerged from the bloodbath stronger than ever. Hitler appointed him Commander of the Home Army in place of Fromm, while General Guderian took over as Chief of the General Staff.

As more men were forced by torture to reveal the names of fellow conspirators, the arrests and executions went on throughout the remainder of the year, even during Hitler's last great Ardennes offensive in the West.

Here, on 16 December 1944, he launched the 250,000-strong reserve armies, created to repel the 1945 Russian spring offensive, in a desperate attempt to split the Allied forces and drive on to the French coast. When the battle ended on 28 January 1945, the Wehrmacht had lost 70,000 killed, 50,000 prisoners, thousands more wounded as well as 1,600 aircraft and 550 tanks.

Now the thousand-year Reich which Hitler had formerly so fondly evoked in his hypnotic speeches began to topple in dreadful ruin as Soviet armies in the East and the Allies in the West blasted their way across Germany towards Berlin. Hitler ordered a scorched-earth policy, but Speer sabotaged it. In the underground bunkers of the Reich Chancellery in Berlin Hitler lived out these last weeks completely out of touch with reality, ordering his generals to counterattack Soviet forces with armies which existed only in his imagination.

In the strangest way—as commentators of various nations have since remarked—Hitler sustained his personal ascendancy over the High Command, over Himmler and his S.S. and over his personal entourage in the bunker. Even after the Soviets entered Berlin on 22 April 1945 and the end was expected daily, there were no recriminations. A mood of dignified fatalism confronted the approaching doom, emanating in the first instance from Hitler.

In these final days and for the first time in his public life Hitler in one surprising event acted with a supreme lack of egoism and self-interest. His mistress, Eva Braun, the pretty, blonde Fräulein whom he had discreetly kept for so many years, had made a dangerous journey and in a gesture of extraordinary loyalty had joined him in the bunker, determined to share his fate and stay with him to the end.

On 29 April 1945, when it was clear from the vibrations of Soviet bombs and artillery in the streets near the bunker that the end was only a matter of hours away, Hitler and Eva Braun were married in a civil ceremony which, almost on her last day, gave Eva what she had wanted so much, the status of Adolf Hitler's wife.

Afterwards, Hitler dictated a personal will and testament to one of his secretaries. Of his sudden marriage he declared: 'As I did not consider that I could take the

A crowd of hungry Germans loot a freight train in Frankfurt as civil order collapses after Germany's defeat in the summer of 1945.

responsibility, during the years of struggle, of contracting a marriage, I have now decided, before the end of my life, to take as my wife the woman who, after many years of faithful friendship, of her own free will entered this city, when it was already practically besieged, in order to share my fate. At her own desire, she goes to death with me as my wife. This will compensate us for what we have both lost through my work in the service of my people.

'I myself and my wife—in order to escape the disgrace of deposition or capitulation—choose death,' he affirmed, in an obvious reference to their suicide pact. 'It is our wish to be burned immediately in the place where I have carried out the greater part of my daily work in the course of my twelve years' service to my people. What I possess belongs—in so far as it has any value to the Party, or, if this no longer exists, to the State. Should the State be destroyed no further decision on my part is necessary ...'

Hitler's final hours were apparently marked by candour and forthrightness. There was no secrecy, no hush, no solemnity. At about dawn on 30 April he assembled his staff, who knew of his intended suicide, and bade them goodbye. Later, while the soldiers and servants danced and sang in the canteen, he went ahead with his final arrangements. It was an extraordinary scene. His pet dogs were destroyed. Relatively calm and self-possessed, he sat down and ate luncheon, and afterwards said a last goodbye to the two men who had stayed with him to the end, Josef Goebbels and Martin Bormann.

At about 3 p.m. he rejoined in their private room the woman who was now Eva Hitler. Soon afterwards there was the sound of a shot. Hitler was found shot through the head and nearby was the body of Eva, dead through poison. Both of them were immediately cremated with petrol. Goebbels poisoned his six children the next day, then ordered an S.S. man to shoot him and his wife. Martin Bormann escaped and vanished into the ruins of Berlin.

Admiral Doenitz, whom Hitler had named as his successor, proclaimed his succession on 2 May 1945,

opened negotiations with General Eisenhower and negotiated the unconditional surrender which General Jodl signed on 7 May 1945 at Eisenhower's Rheims headquarters. Two days later, in Berlin, Keitel signed the capitulation. Himmler, whose arrest as a traitor Hitler had ordered on 28 April for negotiating with the Allies, was captured by a British patrol on 23 May. A few hours later he killed himself with cyanide, and, dying as *Reichsführer-S.S.*, set his final seal upon the destruction of the world's most sinister order, which the Third Reich's military defeat had already inflicted.

Hitler had sown seeds of the deepest hatred between Nazis and Communists in his teaching and in the cruelty and mass murder he had launched in Russia. Now it was the turn of the Soviets. Nazism reached its end in a Berlin turned into a battleground of unparalleled violence, fire and brutality as the Soviet forces dealt blows of destruction and revenge. It was as if the Satanic essence of Nazism shone through the flames and the ruins.

From 20 November 1945 to 1 October 1946 the Nuremberg International Tribunal tried 24 members of the Nazi hierarchy as war criminals, accusing them of crimes 'against Peace, War Crimes and Crimes against Humanity ...' Von Papen, Schacht and Hans Fritsche were acquitted. Twelve were sentenced to death, Bormann in his absence. Goering poisoned himself shortly before he was due to be executed. Ribbentrop, Streicher, Keitel, Kaltenbrunner, Frank, Frick, Jodl, Rosenberg, Sauckel and Seyss-Inquart were hanged. Von Schirach and Speer were sentenced to 20 years, von Neurath to 15 and Admiral Doenitz to 10 years. Lesser lights, such as obscure S.S. murderers, were tried before the various Allied Military Tribunals.

Many Nazis thus paid with their lives for the misery and death they unleashed upon the world in seeking to clamp their creed of hatred and domination upon its peoples.

Can the mystery of the evil of Nazism be explained? Was there a Satanic nucleus at the heart of it? One interpretation of its nature that should be mentioned is the link between Nazism and the alleged attachment to black magic and occultism of Hitler and his inner circle, including Goering, Himmler, Goebbels, Ley and, in the early days, Dietrich Eckart and Professor Karl Haushofer.

Hitler, according to what may seem to many people a far-fetched belief, was the medium through whom contact was made with supernatural powers of evil. Hermann Rauschning, who observed Hitler with a cold and analytical eye, declares that he was a medium, 'possessed by forces outside himself—almost demoniacal forces'. Rudolf Olden, political editor of the *Berliner Tageblatt* in the days of Nazism's rise to power, remarked how the overwhelming, almost superhuman Niagara of words that poured forth during Hitler's speeches sometimes reached a climax during which he literally 'spoke in tongues' and seemed possessed. André François-Poncet, French Ambassador to Berlin, also referred to this apparent demoniacal possession.

Hitler's mediumistic powers supposedly provided the link with Satanic forces which spoke through him and led

The face of defeat: a crumpled and apprehensive
Goering faces his American captors.

to the black magic and occult practices in the inner circle of Nazi leaders. Rauschning also reports in *Hitler Speaks* a warning given to Hitler by a percipient woman in his circle, one of the few who dared to speak forthrightly to him. 'My Führer, do not touch black magic,' she said. 'As yet both white and black magic are open to you. But once you have embarked upon black magic it will dominate your destiny. It will hold you captive. Don't choose the quick and easy successes.

'There lies before you the power over a realm of pure spirits. Do not allow yourself to be led away from your true path by earth-bound spirits which will rob you of creative power.'

Apparently Hitler disregarded the warning and was dominated by the evil forces, who, bribing him with early successes, forced him along the path of their own choosing towards an inferno which destroyed him, split Germany and impoverished Europe and Britain for two decades.

To believe this theory one must suspend rational judgement, but are there not in any case fields of human experience which it cannot explain? And does not this theory of Hitler being dominated by evil supernatural forces throw light for the first time on the reason for Auschwitz, Treblinka, the deaths of six million Jews, the plan to murder 33 million of the Slav population of Russia, the readiness to sacrifice three or four million of Germany's young man-

hood in war and, finally, the long-term aim, reported by Fabian von Schlabendorff, for the total and permanent destruction of Christianity throughout the world?

In Ernst Röhm's expressive phrase, the Nazis were out to lift the world off its hinges, to destroy the power both of the proletariat and the middle classes and to found a new order of society to accord with the commands of the demonic voices which spoke through Hitler. 'I will tell you a secret,' he told Rauschning. 'I am founding an Order ... In my *Ordensburgen* there will stand as a statue for worship the figure of the magnificent, self-ordaining God-Man ...' Hitler at this point checked himself with the remark that there were matters of which even he must not permit himself to speak.

Until more research has been devoted to the issue of Hitler's link with supernatural forces the subject must remain a closed book. Perhaps we should content ourselves with the words of General von dem Bach-Zelewski, at the Nuremberg International Tribunal: 'You will never know the whole truth.'

Jubilant Allied troops pose among the ruins of the Chancellery after the fall of Berlin in May 1945.

Acknowledgments

Hutchinson Publishing Group Ltd, and Houghton Mifflin Co.:
From *Mein Kamp* translated by Ralph Manheim. Reprinted by permission.

Hutchinson Publishing Group Ltd:
From *I Knew Hitler* by Kurt Ludecke. Reprinted by permission.

Oxford University Press:
From *The Speeches of Adolf Hitler* edited by Norman H. Baynes. Reprinted by permission.

Laurence Pollinger Ltd, and G. P. Putnam's Sons:
From *Austrian Requiem* by Kurt von Schussnig. Reprinted by permission.

The publishers are grateful to the following for the illustrations reproduced in this book:

Associated Press 17 (T), 82 (L), 132; Barnaby's Picture Library 136 (B); Bavaria Verlag 7 (T), 20, 24–5, 33 (T), 46, 48 (T), 80 (L), 91, 102, 130 (T); Camera Press 121, 138 (BR); Central Press 7 (B), 29 (R), 87, 88 (L), 88 (R), 90 (B), 118–19 (B), 119 (R), 124 (T), 137, 156, Contents Page; Copress 66–7; Deutsche Fotothek Dresden 11 (T), 12 (B); Eupra Press 27 (B), 89, 118 (L), 122, 127, 147 (R), 150 (T), 150 (B); Fox Photos 84 (R), 155; Grosser 119 (C); Imperial War Museum 8–9, 13 (TR), 28 (R), 57, 75 (T), 82 (R), 95, 140 (B), 154; Keystone Press Agency 14, 15 (B), 17 (B), 27 (T), 40–1, 71, 84 (L), 92 (TL), 94, 98 (B), 104–5 (T), 117 (B), 130 (B), 136 (T), 142 (C), 143 (T), 157; Kobal Collection 44 (TL), 44 (TR), 45 (C), 45 (B); Paul Popper 6, 15 (TL), 16 (TR), 21 (T), 22–3, 34, 38 (T), 54 (TL), 56, 59 (T), 73 (B), 74 (B), 76 (TL), 78 (TL), 79, 98 (T), 112, 118 (C), 120, 134, 146 (L), 153 (L); Radio Times Hulton Picture Library 31, 133; Snark International 13 (TL); Staatsbibliothek Bildarchiv 11 (B), 12 (T), 15 (TR), 18 (L), 18 (R), 35, 48 (B), 50, 53 (T), 53 (B), 62, 63, 64, 80 (C), 99, 135 (T), 138 (T), 138 (BL), 141, 143 (B), Half-Title Page; Süddeutscher Verlag 17 (C), 70, 74 (T), 81 (B), 103, 135 (B); Syndication International 144; Topix 126 (B); Ullstein Bilderdienst 21 (B), 26 (T), 28 (L), 37, 38 (B), 51 (T), 58 (TR), 60, 72 (L), 72 (R), 73 (T), 75 (B), 77 (T), 78 (TR), 81 (T), 83, 86, 90 (T), 93, 96, 100 (R), 104–5 (B), 111 (T), 111 (BL), 113 (B), 115, 117 (T), 123, 124 (B), 125, 129, 131, 147 (L), 153 (R); Victoria and Albert Museum 80 (T); H. Roger Viollet 10, 16 (TL), 33 (B), 36, 39, 45 (T), 47, 52, 54 (TR), 59 (B), 78 (B), 113 (T), 146 (R); Peter G. Wickman 28 (C), 58 (TL), 85 (CR), 142 (L); Wojskowa Agencia 140 (T); Zeitgeschichtliches Bildarchiv 26 (B), 29 (L), 32, 42–3, 61, 65, 68–9, 72 (C), 76 (B), 85 (B), 100 (L), 101 (T), 101 (B), 106, 107, 108, 111 (BR), 126 (T), 148 (B), 151, 152, Title Page.

Bibliography

W. Bartoszewski. *War Crimes in Poland*, 1961

N. H. Baynes. *The Speeches of Adolf Hitler*, 1942

K. D. Bracher. *The German Dictatorship*, 1971

A. Bullock. *Hitler, A Study in Tyranny*, 1952, 1973

T. H. Burden. *The Nuremberg Party Rallies*, 1967

W. Churchill. *The Second World War*, Vols. I–VI, 1948–54

J. C. Fest. *The Face of the Third Reich*, 1970

A. François-Poncet. *The Fateful Years*, 1949

J. Goebbels. *The Diary of Josef Goebbels*, 1925–6

K. Heiden. *Der Führer*, 1944

A. Hitler. *Mein Kampf*, translated by J. Murphy, 1939; *Mein Kampf*, translated by R. Mannheim, 1969

E. Kogon. *The Theory and Practice of Hell*, 1950

K. Ludecke. *I Knew Hitler*, 1938

E. von Manstein. *Lost Victories*, 1958

R. Manvell and H. Frankel. *Heinrich Himmler*, 1965

W. Maser. *Hitler*, 1973

A. S. Milward. *The German Economy at War*, 1965

A. J. Nichols. *Weimar and the Rise of Hitler*, 1968

R. Olden. *Hitler, the Pawn*, 1936

F. von Papen. *Memoirs*, 1958

H. Rauschning. *Hitler Speaks*, 1939; *Germany's Revolution of Destruction*, 1939

G. Reitlinger. *The Final Solution*, 1953; *The S.S.: Alibi of a Nation*, 1956

F. von Schlabrendorff. *The Secret War against Hitler*, 1966

K. von Schussnigg. *Austrian Requiem*, 1955

W. L. Shirer. *The Rise and Fall of the Third Reich*, 1964

M. Shulman. *Defeat in the West*, 1949

A. Speer. *Inside the Third Reich*, 1970

O. Strasser. *Hitler and I*, 1940

F. Thyssen. *I Paid Hitler*, 1941

H. Trevor-Roper. *The Last Days of Hitler*, 1950

J. W. Wheeler-Bennett. *The Nemesis of Power*, 1953

C. Wrighton. *Heydrich: Hitler's Most Evil Henchman*, 1962

Index